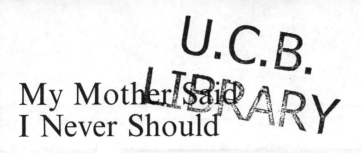

My Mother Said
I Never Should

A play

Charlotte Keatley

Samuel French - London
New York - Toronto - Hollywood

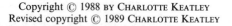

eternal dreams, blood samples
pouring from one glass to the next.
                                    Mandlestam

For

Hilda, Prudence, Susan, Victoria, Nicole
Joan, Jenny, Jane, Michele, Nettie
Judith, Shirley, Nancy
and especially
for Brigid, who made the play happen
and for Mum, who inspires me to communicate,
with love.

MY MOTHER SAID I NEVER SHOULD

Originally premiered at the Contact Theatre, Manchester, on 25th February 1987, with the following cast of characters:

Doris Partington	Joan Campion
Margaret Bradley	Jenny Howe
Jackie Metcalfe	Jane Paton
Rosie Metcalfe	Michele Wade

Director and Dramaturg: **Brigid Larmour**
Designed by **Nettie Edwards**

The play was presented in a revised version, printed here, at the Royal Court Theatre, London, in March 1989, with the following cast of characters:

Doris	Elizabeth Bradley
Margaret	Sheila Reid
Jackie	Jane Gurnett
Rosie	Shirley Henderson

The play was directed by **Michael Attenborough**
Designed by **Tanya McCallin**

The action of the play takes place in Manchester, Oldham and London

CHARACTERS

Doris Partington. Born: Oldham, February 1900. Engaged in 1923. Married Jack Bradley in Oldham, 1924. (Age 5 in child scenes, as in 1905)

Margaret Bradley. Born: Cheadle Hulme, April 1931. Married Ken Metcalf in London, 1951. (Age 9 in child scenes, as in 1940)

Jackie Metcalfe. Born: London, July 1952. (Age 9 in child scenes, as in 1961)

Rosie Metcalfe. Born: Hulme, Manchester, September 1971. (Age 8 in child scenes, as in 1979)

SETTING

The setting should not be naturalistic. The design should incorporate certain objects which remain on stage throughout, such as the piano in Acts I and II, a tub of geraniums, a patch of waste ground. There are no sofas in this play. The setting should simply be a magic place where things can happen.

In the child scenes, each girl is dressed contemporary to her own generation, in the clothes each child wears as a child in the "real" time scenes, e.g. Margaret wears her Christmas frock, Jackie wears her 1961 summer dress.

The interval should occur between Acts II and III.

The playwright will be happy to divulge the secret solution to the Solitaire game to the actresses concerned whenever the play is performed.

ACT I

A patch of wasteground at the end of a terraced street, where children play

Four girls enter each dressed contemporary to her own generation. They hold hands and spin round fast, singing

> My Mother said I never should,
> Play with the gypsies in the wood,
> If I did, she would say,
> Naughty girl to disobey!

They split off from the circle. Jackie watches the others

Rosie (*chanting*) What are little girls made of? (*Coaxing Doris to answer*) Ssh ...
Doris Sugar—and—(*Effort*)—spice ... ?
Margaret And ...
Doris (*desperately stuck*) And?
Margaret All things Nice.

Doris squirming, doesn't want to repeat it

Jackie (*can't bear it any longer*) Let's kill our mummy.
Margaret Whose mummy?
Doris Whose mam? (*Copying*)
Rosie Yes, whose mum?
Jackie All our mummys if you like?
Rosie Who's going to do it?
Margaret (*to Jackie*) Dare you!
Doris ... Dare you ...
Jackie We'll all do it.
Margaret It's my teatime ...
Rosie How?
Jackie I dunno ... Boiling oil.
Doris ... Dare you ...
Margaret Shut up, baby.
Jackie Tell you what—
Rosie What—
Jackie I've got a penknife. I've been keeping it for something special.
Rosie You pinched it off Jimmy Tucker!
Jackie And we'll get some string, and take Mummy down by the railway line where there's a hole in the fence, and I think you have to put a stake through her heart.

Rosie We couldn't do them *all*. (*Pause*) We haven't got enough string.

Jackie Just ours, then. (*Conspiratorially*) They're not in our gang. Also they don't count because they're babies. They can do their own mummys when they're old enough.

Margaret Do mine!—I don't like blood ...

Jackie Lucy Parker cut her finger off at school.

Margaret I'll be sick.

Jackie Only the top bit. (*Pause*) Like a flap.

Doris ... Flip flop flap ...

Rosie(*bending to Doris*) Do you want us to do your mum?

Margaret She's too young to know.

Jackie She's got no daddy: if we do her mummy, she'll be an orphan and then we'll be responsible.

Margaret Her mummy's all right—She gave us lemonade.

Pause

Rosie ... She'll split on us though. Then we'll be outlaws.

Jackie Go away, baby.

Doris cries

Jackie Go on. Go home. (*She pushes Doris away*) Tea? Teatime.

All Teatime, teatime!

Doris goes

Jackie Piggy.

Margaret She'd only cry when she saw the blood. Me. I'm not having any babies.

Rosie How d'you know?

Margaret Well I'm not getting married.

Rosie (*after a pause; thinking*) Well it still might grow.

Margaret What?

Rosie The seed. The baby seed, inside you.

Margaret It can't! Can it?

Jackie has been arranging sweet wrappers

Rosie What are you doing?

Jackie Voodoo. We need bits of her fingernail and hair and stuff.

Rosie ... She might haunt us ...

Jackie You don't know *anything*, do you.

Rosie is subdued. Margaret comes to look

Margaret What's that for?

Rosie Voodoo, you wally.

Jackie We're going to have a seance. To call up ... spirits from beyond the grave.

Margaret We do that at school.

Jackie Do you?

Margaret On Fridays. Take buttercups apart and count their ... sta—stay— ... bits.

Jackie Shh! Hold hands.

They obey

You have to repeat after me.

Margaret | After me.
Rosie |

The lights dim a bit

Jackie (*deepening her voice*) We call up the spirit of—Granny!

Rosie | Gran!
Margaret | Granny!

Jackie Who died three years ago last Wednesday. And lived in Twickenham. Amen.

Margaret | Amen.
Rosie | Amen.

The lights darken

Margaret ... It's getting dark ...

Rosie ... What happens now? ...

Jackie (*in a deep voice*) YOU from beyond the grave! Tell us how to kill mummy!

The lights almost black-out. Silence

YOU from beyond the grave, tell us—

Margaret and Rosie see something, scream and run off

The figure of Doris, now as Gran, appears upstage, walking slowly towards them

Jackie Mummy! Mummy!

Jackie runs off

Doris continues to walk forward, oblivious of the earlier action. She removes a dustsheet of World War Two black-out material from a large object which it has been completely covering. It is a baby grand piano. Margaret is crouching underneath it, hidden from Doris by a pile of bedding also under the piano. Doris begins to dust the piano as the lights rise for Scene Two and the wireless begins to play

SCENE 2

Cheadle Hulme, Christmas 1940

Doris is forty. Margaret is nine. The sense of a large front room, with austere decor. French windows. No Christmas decorations except for a vase of white wax Christmas roses with a red bow, on the baby grand piano

Doris dusts the piano lovingly. The wireless plays George Formby's "Chinese Laundry Blues". A pile of bedding is folded under the piano

Doris (*singing along*) "Oh Mr Wu, he's got a naughty iron that flickers you ought to see it wobble when he's ironing ladies"—
Margaret Knickers.
Doris Margaret? Margaret! Where—(*She goes to the wireless and switches it off*)—Come out!
Margaret (*from the bedding under the piano, with a doll in her hands*) WHO was that?
Doris I have to listen to the wireless. In case Mr Churchill makes an announcement. It is my duty.
Margaret Knickers.
Doris Margaret. Come Out!
Margaret It was Sukey.

Doris walks around the piano

Margaret (*singing, at first softly*) "Sukey take it off again, off again, *off again*. SUKEY TAKE IT OFF AGAIN—"

Doris pulls Margaret out from under the piano by her arm

Doris Never, never!
Margaret Sukey! (*She comforts the doll*)
Doris I've told you before!
Margaret You've hurt Sukey's arm! Torn her dress!
Doris (*shakes her*) *Will* you listen!
Margaret (*to the doll*) Sukey, don't cry. Mummy will cuddle you.
Doris I shall have to tell Father.

Pause

Margaret Sorry.
Doris Pardon?
Margaret I'm very sorry, Mummy.
Doris Mother.

Pause

Margaret Mother.
Doris And you've spoiled your frock. I'd just pressed that.
Margaret Haven't! ... Yes I have.
Doris Have you done your practice?
Margaret (*trying a lie*) Yes. Bits of Chopin and Ten Very Easy Carols.

Doris removes the carol music from the piano and replaces it with a piece of Beethoven music

Doris You ought to be on Beethoven now, not nursery rhymes. The amount we're paying for your tuition.
Margaret You're not throwing them away?!

Doris Of course not. They'll go to St Mark's jumble. Let me hear Beethoven's Minuet in G. Margaret. Have you washed your hands?

Margaret holds out her hands, palms up and then palms down

Good girl.

Margaret sits down at the piano and starts to play, very shakily, Beethoven's Minuet in G. She sways from side to side

What on earth are you doing, Margaret?
Margaret I'm swaying with passion. Like that fat lady in the Hallé Orchestra.
Doris We'll have less passion and more perseverance, please.

Margaret resumes playing

The sound of an air-raid siren, distant

She plays on

Doris nods to emphasize the tempo. Margaret looks at Doris and keeps on playing. Margaret is still playing, but stumbling. Eventually

That will do nicely for this evening, Margaret. I think we shall get under the piano, now. Close the lid.
Margaret Next Door have got a proper Andersen shelter.
Doris (*miffed*) So shall we, presently. Father's been to the Depot but they've run out, had a pre-Christmas rush.

They arrange blankets, an old-fashioned sleeping bag, a stone hot water bottle and a bolster. Margaret hangs her Christmas stocking on the piano

Help Mother make the bed.
Margaret Watch out Sukey, here comes a big fat bomb! Wheee! Eeee—oww–d–d–d–d—
Doris Margaret!
Margaret Well it looks like a bomb.
Doris It's a bolster.
Margaret I *know*, I—Sukey thinks—

The distant rumble of aeroplanes which continues through the rest of the scene

S . . . Sukey wants a Christmas stocking too. She's not very . . . brave.
Doris You got to the other side and help me tuck the blankets in.
Margaret Where's my gas mask?
Doris Here, see I'll put it by the bolster.
Margaret Where will you and Father sleep?
Doris In the hall.
Margaret Why?
Doris I think the ground floor is safest.
Margaret Why?
Doris (*pause*) Sometimes the bombs make the houses shake a little. They make holes in the roof. Nothing will fall on you there.

Margaret Except the piano. (*Pause. Quietly*) Gillian's mother and father sleep in one bed, not two.
Doris (*rhetorically*) Are you getting into bed?

Margaret isn't

Margaret Yes.

The lights fade from here on

Margaret gets into bed

Sukey—! (*She holds the doll tight*)
Doris Tuck you up ... tuck you in.
Margaret Will Father Christmas know I'm under the piano?
Doris I expect so—see Margaret, you're a parcel and I'm wrapping you up!
Margaret *And* they've got a Christmas tree. Why can't *we* have a tree with candles? Can't we?
Doris *Mayn't we.*
Margaret Mayn't we?
Doris No. Pine needles cause a mess. Besides, candles are dangerous.
Margaret Can Hitler see them?
Doris You never know.
Margaret (*impressed*) Does Hitler fly over our house?
Doris Have you said your prayers?

The lights are very dim now

Margaret No.
Doris (*going*) I'll say night-night then.
Margaret Stay a minute!

Doris pauses. Margaret doesn't know how to keep her

Do you and Father say your prayers? (*Pause*) Do you?
Doris Father does. I think that does very nicely for the both of us.
Margaret Do *you*?
Doris I'm saying goodnight now.
Margaret Will we win the war?
Doris Not if you don't keep quiet and go to sleep. (*She goes to the door*)
Margaret What do you mean? (*Pause*) Gillian says parts of Manchester there's nothing left, just bricks squashed. She says people get squashed under there. (*Silence*) Mother? ...
Doris Father will be home soon.
Margaret (*calling*) Mother—(*Pause*) Mummy ... (*Pause*) What happens when you die?
Doris (*after a long pause*) I'll bring you some cocoa presently.

Doris exits

The sound of aircraft fades

Margaret Sssh Sukey Ssh!—No, I won't hold you. You ought to go to sleep now, by yourself. You don't need your Mummy to kiss you. You're eight years old.

The lights black out

> *Margaret exits taking the Christmas stocking, the bedding, hot water bottle and gas mask with her. She leaves the doll lying a little way from the piano*

> *Jackie takes her place under the piano*

> *Doris returns, with a floral overall over her clothes*

The lights come up bright

Birdsong

A May day, it is 1961. Doris is sixty-one; Jackie is nine

Doris Jackie? (*She peers under the piano*) Jackie! What *are* you doing under the piano?

Jackie Seeing what it's like. Mummy says you used to put her to bed under the piano here in the Second World War. And listen to the wireless . . .

Doris Margaret says you read a lot of books.

Jackie Only 'cos she won't let me watch telly. Daddy does. Why d'you call her Margaret?

Doris Because she's *my* little girl. You are always your mother's child my mother used to say.

Jackie She's my mummy.

Doris I'm her mummy.

Jackie Yes but she calls you "Mother". That's different.

Doris How?

Jackie Just is. (*Pause*) You won't tell Mummy about the cup I broke?

Doris It was only Utility.

Jackie What's that?

Doris From the war. (*Pause*) I'll tell her . . . you've been a very good girl. All by yourself, too. (*Pause*) We'll go in the garden and break two jam jars presently.

Jackie Why?

Doris Everything goes in threes. If you break one thing, more is sure to follow.

Jackie Is that true?

Doris So they say.

Jackie Who's they? (*She strokes the piano*) Why has your bath got feet? This is very old wood.

Doris As old as your Grandparents. It's the first thing we bought with our savings after we got married.

Jackie Yes it is a bit old fashioned.

Doris (*rubbing the wood*) Classical.

Jackie (*stroking the white flowers in the vase on the piano*) Are these plastic?

Doris No! *Wax.*

Jackie Can't you afford plastic?

Doris I've had those *years*. Since your mother was a little girl.

Jackie We've got new kitchen chairs with yellow seats.

Doris (*disapproving*) Yes. Your mother likes all these new Formicas, doesn't she.

Jackie When you spill your lunch you can wipe it off straight away. *All* our furniture's new. Poor old Gran. It's all old here, isn't it?
Doris It was new once.

Pause. Jackie contemplates this

Jackie Do you know something?
Doris What?
Jackie I like your old house.
Doris (*pleased*) You tell your mother.
Jackie Why?
Doris Do it for me.
Jackie (*musing*) We don't have a larder you can hide in, either.
Doris We'll make fairy cakes, then we can give Margaret tea when she arrives.

Pause

Jackie Lucy Parker in my class can do the hoola hoop to a hundred.
Doris And later on I'll teach you how to say grace, in French.
Jackie What for?
Doris (*holds out her hand*) Come along, let's go and find Mrs Beeton.

Jackie hugs Doris. Doris hesitates for a second, then bends and embraces Jackie

Kiss your old granny, then.

Jackie kisses Doris. Doris kisses Jackie

Jackie It's much nicer here.

They go off together

The lights dim again

Doris enters, without her overall, dressed as at the beginning of the scene. Margaret is not there, but the doll lies a little way from the piano. Doris carries a Utility-ware mug

Doris Margaret? I brought you some cocoa.

The sound of distant planes

Margaret? Are you asleep? . . . Dear? (*Silence*) Well then. You'll just have to drink it cold in the morning. (*She sees the doll and picks it up. As she goes*) Can't waste good sugar and cocoa.

Doris exits

SCENE 3

The wasteground. A secret place which only children can get to

Two cats wail like babies

Rosie runs in carrying a plastic carrier bag with rattling objects in it. She finds the bits of sweet wrappers from the voodoo in Scene One. She arranges them in the pattern which Jackie used. She looks at them for a moment, picks them up. She climbs to her secret hide and scatters the pieces, watches them fall

Doris runs in

Rosie Mum's got the curse. (*Pause*) Maybe we did it!
Doris (*pause*) What curse?
Rosie *The* curse.
Doris Oh. Yes ... How d'you know she's got it?
Rosie You can tell.
Doris How?
Rosie Just can. Mum's been cross with me all morning.
Doris So what?
Rosie Well you'd be cross if you'd been cursed. (*Pause*) Like in that story. She might turn into something.
Doris Will she die?
Rosie You have the curse until you're an old, old lady.
Doris Then what?
Rosie Then it stops. (*Pause*) Then you die.
Doris Did she prick her finger and bleed?
Rosie Dunno. She might've, but I didn't see any blood.
Doris Cross your heart she's got the curse?
Rosie And hope to die. (*She lowers her voice conspiratorially*) We were in the ABC having buns. Mum said she was going to the Ladies. When she came back, she said, "We'd better go quickly, I've got the curse". (*Pause*) So I went into the Ladies to have a look ... and sure enough, on the wall there it was!
Doris (*frightened*) What?
Rosie The little heart-shaped drawing!!

Stunned silence

Doris Oh ...
Rosie I thought she'd been looking different. Sort of oldish in her face.

They savour the moment. Then, fast

Rosie |
Doris | (*together*) Doctors and nurses!
Doris Bags be nurse!
Rosie I'll be doctor. (*Pause*) Who'll be patient?
Doris All right. I'll be patient and you be doctor and then it's my turn.
Rosie I've brought our kit.

Rosie opens the plastic carrier. Rosie takes out a large sanitary towel and fits it over her head with the loops over her ears

Good morning Mrs Bradley what seems to be the trouble can you take your knickers off please.
Doris I don't think we ought.

Rosie You been telling?

Doris (*pause*) No.

Rosie You have.

Doris I think Mam knows. What we do ...

Rosie How, dummy?

Doris (*pause*) She says she can see inside my head.

Rosie We'll just have to pretend, then. (*She coughs*) Can you lie down please not very nice for the time of year is it.

Doris hesitates, then lies down

    Tut tut tut.

Doris Is it very bad?

Rosie I'll just have to feel it.

Doris (*jumping up*) Don't touch!

Rosie But you like it.

Doris I might catch a babby.

Rosie I think you've got one already.

Doris That's my husband's fault, you can't trust him.

Rosie How is your husband?

Doris Oh he's upped and gone.

Rosie Oh I am sorry.

Doris I'm not. You must drop by for a cuppa. That's enough now, your turn.

They swap positions: Doris wears the sanitary towel, Rosie lies down

Rosie Will you have to stethoscope me?

Doris Oh yes all right. (*She takes a kitchen funnel from the carrier bag and listens to Rosie's stomach*)

Rosie Can you hear anything?

Doris Yes I think the babby's coming out.

Rosie Shall I tell my husband?

Doris No not yet. There's no cause for alarm.

Rosie Will it hurt?

Doris PUSH! It's like doing a big poo. Then the baby pops out.

Rosie You know the yellow nightie we hid? Mam wore that when I was born. It's got a dark red stain on it.

Doris It's not, it's brown.

Rosie Blood dries up. When it's very old.

Doris Truly? Let's go and look.

Rosie When a baby's born they cut the cord.

Doris What's that?

Rosie It joins the baby to its Mummy.

Doris (*contemplates*) Let's be babbies tomorrow.

Rosie No, it's weddings tomorrow.

Doris Why?

Rosie You have to get married first.

Black-out

SCENE 4

Raynes Park, London, May 1969

The garden of Ken and Margaret's suburban semi

Jackie is nearly eighteen, wears flared jeans with sewn-on badges; Margaret is thirty-eight, wears a flowered apron and carries a tea towel

Jackie sits on the swing beneath the cherry tree with her red transistor blaring "All You Need Is Love"

Margaret comes from the house, flustered

Margaret I should never have let you go to that party in Hammersmith!

Jackie Please, Mummy, leave me alone.

Margaret You said you were staying with his parents!

Jackie We were. But they didn't mind us sleeping together. Not everyone has your hang ups.

Margaret Oh you can wound me sometimes, Jackie!

Jackie You sound like Granny now. (*She switches off the radio*)

Margaret What am I going to tell Daddy?

Jackie If you want me to behave like an adult, then stop treating me like a child!

Margaret (*pause*) You don't know what might happen.

Jackie I might fall in love.

Margaret (*trying to ignore this*) You can get pregnant the first time, you know.

Jackie Thanks for telling me now.

Margaret Well if you'd come to me and said—

Jackie Well I did say I wanted to have a talk with you, actually, and you said "Tell me while we go round the garden centre", don't you remember? (*A slight pause*) Anyway, you can't scare me, because I'm on the pill. OK?

Margaret Since when?

Jackie Since before Neil and I went away at half term. You knew that because you've been reading my diary.

Margaret (*momentarily caught*) Well I've no idea, you might be on drugs, anything! (*She collects herself*) I know I'm going to sound like an old fuddy duddy, ... but ... (*She's stuck*) It's a serious step you've taken, you've no idea—

Jackie It was no big deal. It was a relief to get it over with. I cried afterwards. Then I laughed. I expect it's better with someone you're in love with.

Margaret You could have waited.

Jackie Why?

Margaret I had to.

Jackie That's it, isn't it? (*She gets up and goes to the house*)

Margaret If this affects your A levels!

Jackie (*stopping*) What?

Silence. Margaret has nothing to say

I'm going to make a phone call. Phone Neil.

Jackie goes into the house

Pause. Margaret picks up the transistor

Margaret I had an admirer. He took me to dinner. I'd never eaten oysters before.—Wouldn't let me see the bill, that sort of man. I was sure Ken could tell, when I got in. I'd had my hair done, on a Wednesday. (*Pause*) Ten years ago.

Black-out

SCENE 5

The garden of Doris's house in Cheadle Hulme, Manchester 1961

Jackie is nine, Margaret is thirty, Doris is sixty-one

The sound of a lawnmower, off right

Doris enters with a chair and a rug, and arranges them on the grass. She glares, off right

Doris (*calling*) Jack! JACK!

The lawnmower sound stops

Are you coming to have tea with us? Ken and Margaret can't stop long.

Pause. The lawnmower sound starts up

(*Shouting*) Well you'd better do round the front, I don't want grass clippings in our tea.

The lawnmower fades away to right

And mind my lily of the valley!

Doris exits to the house

Jackie enters, holding a painting, and paint pot, leading Margaret by the hand followed by Doris, carrying a tea tray

Jackie And I've been doing the pear tree. Look! (*She shows Margaret the painting*)
Margaret Oh that's lovely, darling!
Jackie Grandad let me use his real paints.
Doris He's been teaching you, hasn't he?
Jackie Did you know shadows are purple?
Doris Have you said hello properly?
Jackie (*hugging Margaret*) Are you better?
Margaret Better? (*She looks at Doris*) Mother ...
Jackie Where's Daddy?
Margaret He's gone to fill up the car with petrol.

Doris That chair's for you.

Margaret No, really.

Doris The rug will do quite nicely for me. (*She sits*) Sit down and have some tea.

Margaret Oh we mustn't, I said to Ken we'd be ready to leave as soon as he comes back.

Doris Her bag is packed and in the hall.

Margaret If we stay for tea we won't get home to London till way past Jackie's bedtime.

Jackie I don't mind.

Doris Jackie made the cakes. Didn't you dear?

Pause. Margaret gives in to pressure and sits

Margaret All right, Mother. And what have you been doing, darling?

Jackie I broke a cup and then we broke two jam jars.

Margaret Oh dear.

Doris Jackie's been an angel.

Jackie (*offering the cake*) Have the yellow one with the smartie.

Doris I hope you've been taking the iron tablets, dear.

Margaret resists the temptation to answer back

Margaret (*to Jackie, for the cake*) Thank you.

Jackie (*saying grace in French, very fast*) Que Dieu benisse nôtre pain quotidien. Amen.

Pause

Margaret Well this is very nice.

Doris And how was Windermere? Did you drive about much?

Margaret We stayed in a lovely guest house, a bit pricey but Ken insisted I was pampered.

Jackie What's pampered?

Doris Nursed.

Pause. Jackie looks at Margaret. Margaret looks at Doris

Margaret No, pampered is—being spoiled a bit—like you've been, here!

Doris Thank you, Margaret.

Margaret And I brought you some Kendal mint cake! (*She gives it to Jackie*)

Jackie And some for Granny? Never mind Granny, we can share this. (*She breaks it in half and gives half to Doris, then goes back to her painting*)

Doris I hope you didn't do too much walking.

Margaret It rained a lot. Luckily there was a nice lounge with a fire. Time to sit and think. You know, Mother, I thought I didn't want it, till I lost it. (*Pause*) It's been a blessing, you taking Jackie for the week. But I missed you, darling!

Jackie goes and hugs Margaret

Jackie I cried the first night, didn't I Granny, then at breakfast Grandad let me have your old napkin ring.

Margaret (*holding her*) Oh Jackie.

Jackie And your doll. It's like a real baby, it's got real curled-up toes and fingers. I was practising. I bathed it and put it to sleep, and it shut its eyes.

Margaret No! (*She gets up*)

Jackie Mummy—

Doris Jackie—(*She catches hold of her*)

Jackie I didn't break her, I didn't break the doll!

Doris (*comforts*) Ssh ssh—

Jackie You're hurting (*She breaks free and runs off, knocking the paint pot across the painting*)

Doris If you hadn't been so hasty to get that tempting job, you would never have lost the baby.

Margaret (*busying herself with the painting*) It'll dry in the evening sun, it'll be all right.

Doris That's for Jack. He wanted something from his grandchild. (*She takes the painting*)

Black-out

Scene 6

A council flat in Hulme, Manchester, early December 1971

Jackie is nineteen and a half, Rosie is three months, Margaret is forty

A worn piece of rusty red carpet with ashtrays and mugs strewn on it, also the red transistor from Scene four, now worn and battered. The transistor blares out over Rosie's crying. Rosie is in a Moses basket; she should on no account be played by a plastic doll. As the lights rise, Jackie is packing baby clothes into a holdall

Radio (*Manchester DJ*) ... Today's highest temperature is expected to be a cold three degrees, so wrap up warmly. Most roads in the city have been cleared now, but there's still ice and snow on the Pennines, and police are asking motorists leaving Manchester on Northbound routes to drive slowly because of black ice. Meanwhile, here's something from the Rolling Stones to remind you of summer days ... (*"Honky Tonk Woman"*)

Jackie (*packing hurriedly*) I wanted it to look nice and now it won't all go in!

Rosie yells

(*hitting the transistor, which goes off*) Ssh, Rosie, please—

Rosie yells

Shut up!

Rosie stops crying abruptly

(*gently*) Ssh, ssh, there now . . . Where do you get the energy from, yelling all night? (*She bends over the Moses basket and sings a haphazard tune*) My little rabbit, in your little basket . . .

Rosie coos

Sleep, beautiful . . . ssh . . . ,

Rosie makes a little cry as Jackie moves away to pack again

(*Over Rosie again*) Please don't be crying when Mummy and Daddy arrive!—Where's your red sock? (*She picks it up and dangles it over Rosie, who quietens during the rest of this speech*) Look, it fell out! Give me a smile—yes! There. I even washed your red sock. Washed everything, don't want Mummy to think—(*holding back tears*) I've got to clear up, Rosie.—All these ashtrays, Sandra and Hugh last night, they never think about you, do they? (*She picks up an ashtray*)

Margaret (*from off*) Hello?
Jackie Oh shit, the mess—Come in!

Margaret enters

Margaret Hello Jackie.
Jackie (*immediately casual*) Oh, hi Mummy.
Margaret It's not locked!
Jackie I knew it would be you.
Margaret You've been smoking.
Jackie Journey from London OK?
Margaret Not how I remembered, Hulme. All these tower blocks . . .
Jackie Is Daddy—he's not—
Margaret Waiting in the car.
Jackie He didn't mind?—I'm sorry, I couldn't face—
Margaret He understands.

Pause

Jackie This is Rosie, Mummy.
Margaret I—came up the stairs. (*Pause*) Lift is out of order. (*Pause*) Lot of stairs.
Jackie . . . Please.
Margaret (*after a long pause*) Three months.
Jackie Say hello.

Margaret goes to the Moses basket. Pause

Margaret Pretty.
Jackie (*also going to the basket*) You think so?
Margaret You had curly eyelashes like that.
Jackie (*pleased*) Did I?
Margaret Hello Rosie . . . (*She kisses her*)
Jackie Don't wake her!
Margaret Of course not!
Jackie I'm sorry, it's just—

Margaret You think I don't know?

Rosie coos quietly

(*Very tenderly*) Ssh, there now.

Rosie murmurs

Jackie (*turning away*) I've packed her things ... here. (*She gives Margaret the holdall*) And her bottles are in this carrier. There's a bit of powdered milk left—
Margaret Oh you don't need—
Jackie Well what would I do with it?

An awkward pause. Margaret looks through the clothes in the holdall

Margaret I've been to Mothercare. Got some of those new disposable nappies, like you said. Quite different from when you were a baby (*She sees another carrier bag across the room and goes to pick it up*) What about this bag—what a sweet—won't she want this dress with the rabbit on?
Jackie Leave those!—Things she's grown out of.
Margaret Why did you have to try! All by yourself? Didn't you believe me?
Jackie I wanted to see if the theories worked—all those late-night chats ... love and flower power ... (*Pause*) When I came back from hospital everyone had cleared out. You'd think I had VD, not a new baby.
Margaret He should be here with you, your—(*stuck for a word*)—Rosie's father.—You in these flats ...
Jackie (*calmly*) Mummy, I told you. He visits; and sends money. It was my decision.
Margaret Ye~ but you had no idea! I told you, I told you! Nothing, for nearly three months, nothing, since the day she was born, then a phone call, out of the blue,—the potatoes boiled dry!
Jackie You knew I'd phone, one day.

Slight pause)

Margaret Look at you now, a year ago you had everything, you were so excited about the art school, new friends, doing so well—
Jackie (*angrily*) I'll go back! Yes I will, finish the degree, I won't fail both things! Only think about her at night, her cheek against mine, soft and furry, like an apricot ...

Rosie makes a snuffling noise in her sleep

... She'll be happy, won't she? ...
Margaret After you phoned ... after you asked us ... Daddy went upstairs and got your old high chair down from the attic. (*Pause*) Like sisters, he said. A new little sister ... (*She bends down to Rosie*) Aren't you, precious?
Jackie (*panics*) Mummy—she's got to know—I can't come and visit, with her not knowing, I can't!
Margaret Jackie, darling, we can't go over this again—you know as well as I do it would be impossible—
Jackie I don't believe you!

Margaret When she's grown up, you can tell her; when she's sixteen.
Jackie It'll be too late!

Silence

Give me the bags.
Margaret (*gently*) You've got such opportunities.
Jackie Expectations.
Margaret Yes!
Jackie Yours.
Margaret You've got to—
Jackie Why? (*She pulls away the holdall*) Why not just Rosie?
Margaret You've got to go further than me. And somehow Rosie must go
   further than both of us. (*Quietly*) Otherwise ... what's it been worth?

Pause

Jackie Here, take them. (*She gives Margaret the bags*) You haven't told
   Granny and Grandad?
Margaret Not yet. I'll talk to them. (*Tentatively*) Perhaps you could stay
   with them, just till Christmas, while you find a new flat? ... (*She bends to
   Rosie*) My little lamb ... What's this?
Jackie She has to have a red sock to go to sleep.
Margaret You keep one.
Jackie (*putting one sock in her pocket*) Love her for me ...

Margaret picks up the Moses basket

I'll help you to the car.
Margaret It's all right, Daddy will be there. (*She picks up the bags and goes
   to the door*)
Jackie I'll come for Christmas. And visit, lots. (*Pause*) Whenever I can
   afford the fare to London.

Margaret exits with the basket and the bags

Jackie (*calling after them*) Sing to her at bathtime, especially the rabbit song
   ... (*Silence. Pause. She picks up the bag she told Margaret to leave. As she
   pulls out the clothes, she is suddenly hysterically happy. She holds up the
   rabbit dress*)—Wore this the day you first smiled, you wouldn't let go of
   my hair,—do you remember?! (*She holds up another*)—And your first
   bonnet ... (*Gently*) And the shawl ... wrapped you up, like a parcel, the
   day we left hospital; all the way back in a taxi, bringing you home ...
   (*Pause*) Our secrets, Rosie. I'll take care of them. (*Pause. Desperately*)
   You'll never call me "Mummy". (*Silence. She screams*) Rosie! Come
   back!—Mummy, Mummy!

*Black-out. For a moment in the darkness, the sound of a baby crying. In a dim
light we see Margaret rocking a bundle. She comforts the baby with the
following words, until the baby quietens and coos*

Margaret There now, there now, hush! Did you have a nasty dream? My
   precious. Mummy's here now. Mummy's here, Rosie. There now ... Did
   you have a bad dream, Jackie? It's all right. Ssh ... ssh.

*As the lights come up bright for the next scene, Margaret turns and billows out
the sheet which was forming the bundle*

SCENE 7

*The garden of Doris's house in Cheadle Hulme, Manchester, 1951. A hot
August day. A distant rumble of thunder*

*Doris, wearing a sensible beige skirt, and Margaret, wearing ski pants, are
folding sheets. Washing is strewn on the lawn and some is folded in a washing
basket. Doris is fifty-one and Margaret is twenty*

The swish and plop of a tennis game played next door

Doris I'll be glad when they put an end to clothes rationing. These sheets
are quite threadbare in the middle.

The sound of light aircraft going overhead

(*She studies the sky*) RAF from the base at Padgate.
Margaret They're B twenty-nines, not Lancasters!
Doris I'll be glad when they're gone. (*Disdainfully*) Americans. Keep that
sheet off the grass, Margaret, it's not a bridal train.
Margaret Mother! Without them we couldn't have won the—
Doris Are you going to help me fold this sheet, or are you just going to
stand there all afternoon identifying aircraft!
Margaret (*staring at the sky*) Maybe one of them's Ken.

They hold the sheet by the corners and tug

Doris I don't see how it can be, if he's calling in half an hour.

They shake the sheet vigorously

Margaret I can't wait to live in London!

No reply

Ken says he can get a job there. He's frightfully clever.

They balloon the sheet up into the air

I'm in love, Mother.

A distant rumble of thunder

Doris looks up at the sky

Doris It's not going to hold.

Pause

They pull diagonals to stretch the sheet

Margaret And I'm going to learn to type! Ken says it will be helpful if we need a second income. (*As they shake the sheet*) Typing's far more modern than all those useless school certificates. I'll get a *proper* job.

Doris What do you call running a home? (*She looks up at the sky*) I knew we were in for a storm.

Margaret I'm not wasting my life.

Doris (*angry*) Thank you Margaret!

They fold the sheet lengthwise

Pull!

Margaret pulls so hard that Doris lets go and they jerk back from each other

There's no need to snatch it out of my hands! (*Pause*) There see, now you've spoiled it all.

Margaret Well you can pick it up again, can't you!

Pause

Doris picks it up; they resume folding

I'm not going to have a family, babies and all that. Ken and I have decided.

A distant rumble of thunder

Doris It will break, soon.

They fold the sheet lengthwise

And what makes you so sure you can keep Mother Nature at bay?

They close in chest to chest and Margaret gives her corners to Doris, who folds the sheet in half and half again during the following

Margaret (*grandly*) There's THINGS you can get ... I've heard about them.

Doris I'm not talking about that. (*She cradles the folded sheets*) I'm talking about the *desire* ... for little arms reaching up and clinging round your neck. (*She buries her face in the sheet, then holds it out to Margaret to do likewise*) Smell: lavender. From the beds, there. Mother Nature is very hard to fight. It's not just a question of rubber things or what have you.

Margaret "Little arms clinging" ... There, see, that's what I don't want. That's the difference between our generations, Mother.

Doris Well I'm glad to know you've worked it out. Margaret can you sort out Father's socks please?

Margaret (*picking the socks off the grass and pairing them*) You want a nice snapshot for the family album don't you? Proof, to show the neighbours. Well I'm going to be different! Women did so much during the war: there's nothing to stop us now.

Doris Ha!

Margaret You think I'm being selfish, don't you?

Doris I felt a few drops, then. (*Pause*) What makes you think I wanted children?

Margaret Mother!

Doris I had a job once too. I know it was only teaching, but ... (*Pause. To stop herself*) There's an odd maroon one over there on the grass. (*Pause. Warning Margaret*) Of course, Father has absolutely no idea. One would never ... tell him. (*Pause*) There wasn't any choice, then; so I don't know whether it was my need—to love him, if you know what I mean ... or his desire—for a son.

A long pause. Doris bends and picks up a sock

Horrible colours he likes. Not my choice at all ... (*Pause*)

Margaret The garden is always so lovely, Mother. May I take a cutting, off one of your geraniums, to London with me?

Doris Oh Margaret ... why does it have to be London?

The sound of a raucous car horn, which repeats

Oh I do wish people wouldn't do that! Bring down the tone of the neighbourhood!

Margaret It's Ken! He's bought an Austin Healey—it's got a folding roof— you must come and see! I said to honk and I'd move Father's car into the garage so Ken can back into the drive—I'll have a lot of cases to load into the boot.

Doris I must say, Jack asked my mother before there was any talk of weddings.

Margaret Have you still got your posy?

Doris He's reversing straight into my lily of the valley!

Margaret He's not.

Doris He is.

Margaret He's not, just parking.

Doris Curious method of parking.

Margaret That's typical, you think all Americans are brash and wear loud check shirts and chew gum and want to marry English girls. You're just prej— ...

Doris Margaret, that's enough! (*Pause*) After all, he is going to marry an English girl.

Margaret Oh Mother, don't look at me like that with your lips pressed together.

Margaret exits

Doris folds the remaining sheet and puts it in the basket during her speech

Doris Well it's too late now. These smalls are damp. I knew this lovely summer wouldn't last. (*Pause*) I suppose I should get the best service out, for tea.

A rumble of thunder, close

She'll need bed linen. These are all worn out ... Something old, something new. So they say.

Doris picks up the basket of washing and starts towards the house. A crack of thunder, overhead. Doris drops the basket, which spills everywhere. Immediately, the sound of pouring rain on leaves. Doris stands and contemplates the spoiled washing all around as the pouring rain grows louder

Lights fade slowly to black-out

SCENE 8

(This scene was cut from the Royal Court production)

The wasteground. Rosie, skipping, chanting

Rosie   Georgey Porgy pudding and pie,
           Kiss the girls and make them cry,
           When the girls come out to play—

Jackie runs up, one hand behind her back

Rosie stops

Jackie I went to the boys' den.
Rosie You said you wouldn't!
Jackie Only slightly.
Rosie You're out of the gang.
Jackie I got the penknife back.
Rosie I don't believe you.

Jackie takes the penknife from behind her back and holds it out between them

Jackie So there.
Rosie So what.
Jackie I kissed a boy.
Rosie You didn't!
Jackie I did.
Rosie What's it like?
Jackie I think I'm in love.
Rosie How d'you know?
Jackie Because this boy made me cry. Daddy makes Mummy cry and she says it's because she loves him. (*She opens the penknife blade*) Now we can do the Vow.
Rosie (*backing away*) It's too late. You've probably got his seed now and it'll grow and grow and fill you up.
Jackie You're still my best friend.
Rosie Don't talk to me about best friends because I'm never playing with you again.

Pause

Jackie Kissing wasn't as good as best friends.
Rosie Why d'you do it then?

Jackie To get the penknife.

Pause

Rosie You didn't need to kiss a boy. You could have given him some bubble gum.

Jackie I did. He wanted a kiss as well.

Pause. Jackie holds the blade up

   They said I'm a cissy.

Rosie You are.

Jackie holds up her index finger and ceremoniously jabs the tip with the penknife; she studies it

Jackie I'm bleeding.

Rosie Do I do it too?
Jackie Yes.

Rosie takes the knife and stabs her own index finger

Rosie Ready.

They face each other and hold fingertips together and recite

Rosie	Truth is honesty
Jackie	Honesty is true,
	Keep your promise
	And I'll keep you.

They step back and suck their fingers: Jackie puts the penkife away

Jackie You can't ever lie to me now.

Pause

Rosie Can you see into the future?
Jackie (*frightened*) A bit.
Rosie Will you have a look for me?

Pause

Jackie It'll happen anyway. Mummy says don't cross bridges.
Rosie Is that a spell?
Jackie I don't know. She just says it.
Rosie At night?
Jackie I heard her say it to Daddy, in the garage.
Rosie Then it must be a spell.

Pause, then together

Rosie
Jackie   Don't-cross-bridges!

Rosie You mustn't ever break a vow.

Black-out

SCENE 9

A telephone conversation, December 1971, later on the same day as Scene Six

Margaret in Raynes Park, London, aged forty. Doris in Cheadle Hulme, aged seventy-one. Margaret dressed as for Scene Six, with the Moses basket beside her

Doris Hello?
Margaret Hello?
Doris Margaret?
Margaret Mother? Oh I was about to ring you. It's not gone six has it?
Doris Two minutes ago. We've just got the news on.
Margaret Oh dear ... I'm sorry, I was just seeing to ...

Rosie cries in the distance

   ... to Ken.
Doris Is he poorly again?
Margaret Oh, no, no! Well, a slight cold. Very slight.
Doris *You* don't sound too well.
Margaret I'm fine.
Doris You don't look after yourself dear.
Margaret (*pause*) Mother, why did you phone?
Doris Oh, just to see if you were all right ...
Margaret How did you know?
Doris (*matter of factly*) What, dear?

At the same time Rosie cries in the distance again

Margaret puts her hand over the receiver and collects herself

Margaret How's Father?
Doris (*pause*) We've still not seen Jackie.
Margaret She's been ... since when?
Doris Well it's been a year now.
Margaret I've only seen her—slightly ...
Doris I suppose she's busy with her studies.
Margaret Oh yes, very.
Doris Only your Father and I thought she might visit, being in Manchester herself now. She's not moved?
Margaret Well, yes, I'm not sure ...
Doris It was Mothering Sunday last week.
Margaret Didn't you get the cards?
Doris Yes, very nice. (*Pause*) But we used to get a hand-painted one from Jackie.
Margaret Well ... you know how it is, she's got to rebel while she's still a teenager.

Doris What?

Margaret Revise. She's got to revise, for her exams.

Doris I thought we might go and visit her.

Margaret Oh no! I shouldn't ... just yet. She's decorating her new flat.

Doris She should have asked us. I've plenty of furnishings put by that I don't need any more.

Margaret How's Father?

Doris Oh, creeping, creeping. Can't do anything with his hands now of course. A mither he was in, trying to sign the will.

Margaret You said.

Doris So I sold his painting things. Some of those easels he's had since we were first married.

Margaret Mother! Why didn't you tell me? Not the sable brushes?

Doris (*pause*) No. Jack wants Jackie to have them. (*Pause*) Of course I said to him I don't suppose she'll want those, being at a polytechnic. (*Pause*) He sets great store by her, you know.

Margaret I'd like you to come and visit us.

Doris We're coming at Easter. Or don't you want us this year?

Margaret Of course, Mother! I thought perhaps the week after next ...

Doris What is it?

Margaret I can't explain on the phone.

Doris You're not hiding anything from us?

Margaret No!

Doris Good or bad, dear?

Margaret What? Oh. (*A long pause*) Good.

Rosie cries in the distance

Very.

Doris It's not that sofa you were telling us about?

Margaret No, it's ...

Doris Well that's two minutes dear. I'll finish now.

Margaret Yes.

Doris Father will be so pleased to know ...

Margaret What?

Doris About Jackie.

Margaret What?!

Doris Revising for her exams. I'm saying goodnight now.

Margaret Goodnight. (*The line has already gone dead*) Jackie, what are you doing ... !

Black-out on Margaret and Doris

Scene 10

The garden of Ken and Margaret's home in Raynes Park, London, as in Scene Nine, September 1979

Rosie is eight Jackie is twenty-seven, Margaret is forty-eight. The cherry tree has grown, the swing is as in Scene Four. It is Rosie's eighth birthday

Rosie enters, carrying an old spoon and Margaret's doll Sukey from Scene Two. It is a baby doll, now bald except for a few tufts which have been spiked. The doll is unclothed apart from one red sock

Rosie It's my birthday today and it's all gone wrong already. I'm going to bury you, Sukey. Eight is too old for dolls. I want a Sex Pistols T-shirt. Some hope. Unless Jackie brings me one! I'd have buried you ages and ages ago, Sukey, if you hadn't been Mum's. I couldn't care less now if Mum sees me doing this. (*She digs in the cherry-tree tub*) Sukey. Stupid name. Even cutting your hair off it won't go punk. I bet Mum cuddled you and stuff, didn't she? Well I only hug people when I want to, not when it's visitors. (*She holds the doll over her face. Pause*) When I want to I can hug harder than anyone. In the world. (*Pause*) I'm saving it. (*She digs the hole. She lowers the doll over it, then holds it closer to her*) I was going to give you away to the Toy Collection at School, d'you know that? Mummys give their babies away sometimes. They do. (*Pause. She slowly lays the doll in the hole*) Shut up crying. There, see, I'm putting you in this urn. People get buried in urns. (*Covering the doll over with earth*) Jackie'll be here soon. She never cries. No one else at school has a sister whꜜ s a grown-up. I might easily run away with Jackie and live with her. Then you'd be sorry. Sukey. So would Mum. (*Suddenly bright, as if enormously relieved*) I'm going to paint the cherry tree now. — for Jackie.

Rosie lies on the grass painting

Jackie enters with a very lavish birthday cake and candles

Jackie Happy-birthday-to-you! . . . Rosie?
Rosie Why did you buy me one? Mum usually makes me one.
Jackie Thanks.
Rosie I mean, it doesn't look as good as this. And she always makes chocolate because she thinks I like it.
Jackie Why don't you tell her you don't?
Rosie Oh you know Mum. Never listens. I think she just likes making birthday cakes. Even *Dad* gets one!
Jackie Let's light the candles.
Rosie Shouldn't we wait for Mum?
Jackie Oh, yes.
Rosie (*pause*) Has it got drink in it?
Jackie Rum. A bit.
Rosie Mum and Dad never drink anything exciting. You know that funny shaped bottle you brought them from Mexico? It's still in the cabinet.
Jackie Well I brought Mum some Greek lace this time. Sort of thing she wouldn't treat herself to.
Rosie She's so *mean*! D'you know, she wouldn't even buy me a Sex Pistols T-shirt, she says, "No dear, you haven't grown out of last year's summer dresses". As if I could be seen wearing those!

Margaret enters with a tray

Margaret What's that dear? Here we are, celebration drinks! How long is it
  since you were last here, Jackie?
Jackie (*silence*) I don't know. Light the candles, Rosie.
Rosie (*as she lights the candles*) One ... year ... and four months.
Margaret I thought we'd have some of the tequila you brought us, Jackie.
  We keep it for special occasions.
Jackie (*to Rosie*) See.
Rosie Me too?
Margaret A little bit.

Pause. All three watch the candles burn

  Magic.
Jackie I used to wish ...
Margaret (*cutting in*) Blow the candles out.
Rosie I think Jackie wants ...
Margaret Now darling, before it spoils.

A moment while Rosie hesitates

  Blow the candles out.
Rosie (*blowing the candles out*) Done it!

Pause

Jackie Wish, Rosie!
Margaret No, you hold the knife and wish as you cut it ...
Jackie No, you wish *first*!
Margaret No, Rosie and I always ...
Rosie Oh stop it, you two!
Margaret Don't we, Rosie.

Silence

  I'll cut it then. It must have cost Jackie a lot.
Rosie I don't want any now. (*She gets up*)
Jackie Don't go. What's this, Rosie love?
Rosie You mustn't look! I can't paint like you can!
Jackie It's lovely, Rosie.
Rosie 'S not, the sun's running down into the grass.
Jackie It could be abstract, all swirls.
Rosie Don't be stupid! It's mess, even you can see that.
Jackie Can I keep it?
Rosie (*snatching it away*) It's for Mum. Here, Mum. (*She gives it to her*) It's
  gone wrong.
Margaret It's lovely! Thank you, pet.

She and Rosie embrace

  Say sorry to Jackie.

Jackie is watching intently

  (*looking at the painting*) Where shall we put it? The kitchen walls are
  choc-a-block.

Rosie On the fridge.

Margaret (*laughing*) Run and put it there, before someone sits on it, like Daddy did.

Rosie exits

An awkward pause

How's Manchester?

Jackie Fine.

Margaret Working hard?

Jackie Yes.

An uneasy silence

Margaret I've got a full-time job now. too.

Jackie (*pleased*) That's good. I'm hoping to open a gallery of my own in a couple of years, with Simon, if we can get the backing.

Margaret Oh I did like Simon.

Jackie We're not—together anymore.

Margaret (*gently*) It would be nice. Jackie, if you found someone, I know you'll hate me for saying this, but it could be very lonely when you're—

Jackie Mummy—(*She stops*) Simon wanted children, I tried to believe I could start again.—Stupid—I just kept dreaming about Rosie.

A moment

Rosie (*calling*) Mum!—Where's the Blu-Tack?

Margaret (*calling*) In the cupboard with the carrier bags.

Rosie (*calling*) Oh, 's all right ...

Jackie She doesn't need me, does she?

Margaret No.

Rosie runs in

Rosie No what?

Margaret No you don't ride your bike on the main road.

Rosie I do! Me and Zoe Taylor nearly crashed, we were kazooming—

Jackie Well you shouldn't! NEVER, ever—

Rosie runs off

—I'm sorry Rosie, I didn't mean to shout at you—

Silence

I do worry about her getting run over, or getting ill, or lost or attacked, and me not being there ...

Margaret I worry about *you*.

Jackie Still?

Margaret Mothers don't grow out of it.

Jackie hands Margaret a small carefully wrapped package

Jackie Here.

Margaret A present—for me? (*She opens it*)
Jackie It's lace.
Margaret (*turning it over in her hands*) Where was it you were this time?—
Greece? (*Bemused*) I try to imagine what it's like, when you go off on
these trips by yourself, no one else to think about!
Jackie It's from the convent on the island. The nuns have used the same
pattern for a thousand years.
Margaret Thank you dear.

A slight pause

Jackie (*handing Margaret a cheque*) Mummy, I've been given a rise; new
bikes are expensive . . . I want to give you a cheque—
Margaret How dare you! This isn't one of your art deals! (*She snatches the
cheque and tears it up*)

Rosie runs in

Rosie What is it Mum? (*She hugs Margaret. To Jackie*) I hate you! (*She
clings to Margaret*) Mum, I want you to see where I've put my painting
Margaret (*as they go into the house together*) Ssh . . . all right darling.

Margaret and Rosie exit

*Jackie stays sitting a moment. She sees the old spoon and scattered earth, then
goes to the cherry tree in its tub, digs out the doll which Rosie buried, brushes it
down. It is naked except for one red sock. Jackie takes the other red sock from
her pocket and puts it on the doll*

Black-out

ACT II

The large front room of Doris and Jack's house. A french window to the garden and a door to the hall. Dustsheets over boxes and the piano. Snow on a rose bush outside the window. Doris is eighty-two, Margaret is fifty-one, Jackie is thirty, Rosie is eleven

Rosie enters with a flashlight and swings it round

Rosie Grandad? You in here? (*Silence, she listens*) Well if you're listening, I want to tell you that it was pretty stupid, what you did. I mean, leaving the house and stuff to Jackie. Mum and Gran were mega hurt, you know that? (*Pause*) Grandad . . . ? I'd like to know did you do it because you like Jackie best . . . or because you're jealous?

Silence. She listens

Then a rustle: something under a dustsheet moves or falls

Rosie jumps and swings the flashlight round

Mice. (*Pause*) I'm not scared of you, Grandad. It's others who are. You didn't get me.

She switches off the flashlight and goes out to the garden through the french windows, shutting them behind her

Doris carrying a feather duster enters with Jackie, carrying boxes and bin liners. Jackie puts these down and exits

Margaret enters with a bag and rubber gloves

Doris Two months ago Saturday Jack died, and the house hasn't been aired since.
Margaret Well, we can soon put that right, Mother.
Doris I doubt it.

The lights come up suddenly and bright. Doris is startled

Jackie enters

Jackie I turned the power on, and the water.
Doris Oh, I don't think that'll be necessary.
Margaret Mother we have to see to clear up.
Jackie You don't have to worry about bills now, Granny. I've worked it all out. (*To Margaret*) I've backed the van up the drive so we can load things straight in.

Doris My lily of the valley!

Jackie I couldn't see. There's snow over everything. (*She billows the dustsheets up off the piano*)

Doris It was terrible on the motorway driving up.

Jackie Have you had a good time in London?

Doris ... Terrible ... (*She is still referring to the journey*)

Margaret Yes, well we're here now, Mother. Have some tea, I've brought a flask. (*She gets out the Thermos and pours a cup*)

Doris I'm quite all right. You have some.

Margaret I want to get on.

Jackie Sit down while the house warms up.

Doris I don't want to be a nuisance to anyone.

Margaret (*wavering, cup in hand*) Jackie?

Jackie Got sugar in it?

Margaret Yes.

Jackie You know I don't.

Margaret You've got no sense of compromise, have you?

Rosie knocks on the french windows with a white rose

Can't you come round to the front door?

Doris She'll catch her death.

Margaret She never does. (*She lets Rosie in*)

Rosie Look what I found! (*It looks like one of the wax roses in the vase on the piano in Act I Scene Two*)

Margaret A Christmas rose.

Doris It's dead.

Jackie It's not, it's frozen.

Rosie That's dead.

Jackie We could unfreeze it.

Rosie Even you can't organize roses to come alive.

Doris (*going to the french windows*) They should all have been pruned by now ... all blown down by the storms.

Jackie Snow on them looks like flowers.

Rosie (*pulling Doris away from the window*) C'mon, we can't prune them now.

Doris I don't want whoever buys this house to think that Jack and I didn't know about roses.

Jackie (*trying to please*) We can pay to have the garden done, before we sell.

Doris (*stiffly*) All that money, and Jack would never spend a penny of it.

Rosie Mum, can Jackie and I make a snowman?

Margaret Rosie, we've only got today and tomorrow to get this house sorted out. I don't suppose Jackie wants us in her flat any longer than that.

Jackie Mummy, you can stay as long as you like you know that!

Margaret You said you've even been using your bedroom to store paintings.

Jackie That was before the exhibition. Anyway Rosie's room is always ready.

Rosie Mum, can't I stay—

Margaret (*sharply*) Rosie. (*Pause*) Now Jackie, you tell us all where to start. Seeing as Father left you in charge of everything.

Jackie Come on Mummy, that's only because I live in Manchester too. He knew I'd be on the spot to deal with the house.

Margaret I suppose being born in this house doesn't count, Jackie.

Beat

Jackie (*passing a bin liner to Doris*) Granny, you take a bin liner and—

Doris She's going to put it all in dustbins!

Jackie You choose which curtains you'd like from this room, the rest we'll leave for the auction.

Margaret I'll make a start on the crockery then.

Margaret pulls the dustsheet off a dresser. A willow pattern service is on the lower shelves, ornaments and framed photographs above

Rosie OK, don't talk to me.

Margaret Rosie, bring that box over and start scrunching up newspaper for packing.

Rosie (*kicking the box over to Margaret*) Do some chores instead.

Jackie (*going to the dresser*) I'm sure you'll want to keep the willow pattern, won't you, Granny?

Doris Old. Cracked.

They wrap and pack the willow pattern during the following dialogue

Margaret Mother, you sit tight and we'll pass you things to wrap.

Doris I shan't want any of this. Jackie's possessions now, according to the will.

Jackie Granny, you'll need things for the house in Oldham.

Doris It's not a house. It's an End Terrace.

Rosie Come off it Gran, that's a bit mean. Jackie bought you exactly the house you wanted.

Margaret Rosie! Don't be rude.

Rosie Well I think you're both being rude to Jackie. She can't help what Grandad did.

Doris It seems that sixty years of housewifery counted for nothing, in Jack's eyes.

Margaret Your house has always been a gleaming example to us, Mother. Rosie, can you fetch some more newspaper please.

Doris Well Jackie didn't follow it, did she. (*A slight pause*) Jack noticed *her* sort of work, because he was always asking how her painting exhibitions were going. And since Jackie didn't care to visit much, I had to make it up. And as you know, modern art was never my strong point.

Rosie She hardly ever visits us, Gran.

Jackie —I'm always there for your birthdays, Rosie.

Rosie Most of them.

Jackie I try—

Rosie S'OK Jackie, you have to travel lots, and your work's the most important thing, isn't it.

Pause

Margaret Funny how a job was never a good enough excuse for me. I think Father disapproved of it.
Rosie But your job's only typing, Mum. (*A slight pause*) Anyway, Jackie's different she's got no kids.

Pause

There is one mug left at the back of the shelf

What's this vile mug?
Doris That's Utility, Rosie. I used to give Margaret cocoa in that.
Margaret I'd forgotten.
Rosie Mum's always giving us cocoa.
Margaret It's funny, Mother, Jackie and Rosie don't even like cocoa.
Doris You only want what you're denied.

Rosie passes the mug to Jackie, who wraps it

Jackie Oh yes—I broke the handle once—see where Grandad glued it?
Margaret I don't remember.
Jackie Oh—you weren't here.
Margaret Why ever not?
Jackie Well it was the summer you—(*stuck*)—weren't well.
Margaret (*pause*) I don't remember.

Pause. Jackie puts the mug in the box which is now full and tapes it closed

Jackie There's the willow pattern, Granny.
Doris That was my wedding. Was never the set I wanted.

Pause

Jackie Rosie, take Granny into the kitchen and see if there's any pans she'd like to take.
Doris What about the bedrooms?
Margaret What about them, Mother?
Doris Well Rosie will need bed linen.
Rosie What for?
Doris You never know.
Rosie I've got a duvet.
Margaret Rosie.
Rosie I have!
Jackie Rosie, why don't you and Granny go upstairs and sort some sheets.
Doris Come along, Princess.
Rosie I'm not a princess. I'm a punk.—We could get in your old wardrobe, Gran.
Doris Why love?
Rosie 'Cos it's brill for hiding. Come on Gran.

Rosie leads Doris out of the room

Doris I want to know, when did I stop being Granny, and turn into Gran?
Rosie You like it.

Rosie and Doris exit

Pause

Jackie (*to Margaret*) I thought we might have a chat.
Margaret We can while we finish these shelves, can't we.

Jackie does not reply. She fetches the stepladder and puts it up by the shelves

Jackie How's work?
Margaret Fine. How's yours?
Jackie Oh—OK. (*Pause*) I'll climb, and pass you things.

They work

Margaret I read an article at the hairdressers', about a girl who does silk-screen printing, in Sheffield. Rather like you.
Jackie I don't do silk-screen printing. (*Pause. She passes a frame*) What a serious child you were!
Margaret (*looking at the photo*) On the beach at Scarborough. I was six years old. I remember Father wanted a nice one ...
Jackie "The highest standard", he'd always say to me.
Margaret Nineteen thirty-seven. I remember Father kissing me that day, and saying, "You're nearly grown up now". He didn't kiss me after that. (*Pause*) If you left a bit of butter on your plate, it was either Mother on at you about rationing, or Father would tell us again, how he started his business with a tin of boot polish, cleaning gentlemen's shoes on the steps of the Royal Exchange. What that had to do with butter, I really don't know.
Jackie (*lifting down a silver rose bowl*) The rose bowl. "Manchester Business Award, nineteen forty-nine".
Margaret He took me to the Exchange once, to look at his shares. Young women had to wait outside, of course. (*She has a spasm of pain*)
Jackie Mummy—is it upsetting you?—Sit down for a bit.
Margaret (*fighting the pain*) So much to do. (*She continues packing*)

Jackie looks worried

Next shelf, Jackie.
Jackie The pottery duck I made—look.
Margaret Rosie made that.
Jackie No. I made it for Grandad.
Margaret I think I should know.
Jackie Mummy I—

Margaret has another spasm of pain

Please stop doing things for a moment.
Margaret It's just menopause. Cramps ... (*She sits*)

Jackie climbs down

Jackie It shouldn't do that to you. Have you seen a doctor?
Margaret Surgery hours are nine till six. I'm working then.

Pause

Jackie Rosie's very energetic . . .
Margaret She's like you.
Jackie . . . I meant it Mummy, about school holidays.
Margaret And how would you cope, the hours you work?

Pause

Jackie I could time share with Sandra at the City Art Gallery. I asked
her.—She's got two small children now.

Pause

Margaret All Rosie's schoolfriends are in London.

Pause

Jackie It was just an offer. (*Clumsily*) If you ever feel you can't cope—
Margaret What are you suggesting?!
Jackie Mummy, I want to ask you—(*She stops*)

Pause

Margaret What?

They look at each other. A long pause

Jackie Let's get on.

Margaret gets up, Jackie climbs the stepladder

When I've sold this house and invested the money for everyone, you
won't have to work so hard.
Margaret I have to work. There's always something. I don't have your
attitude to the future, Jackie.

Pause

Jackie (*at the top shelf*) That's everything. No, what's this? (*She lifts down
an old chocolate box, opens it*)—Look, a Victorian photograph! The
frame's made of shells . . .

Pause

Margaret That's mother's mother.
Jackie (*excitedly*) Is it? Look at that stiff black dress—and the high collar.
Margaret Goitres. Women over thirty never showed their necks in those
days. Swellings. Hormone problems. No proper medicine to control it.
Jackie Why hasn't Granny ever showed us this?

Pause

Margaret Jack didn't like it. (*Pause*) Mother grew up in what she calls—reduced circumstances . . . Her mother wasn't married.

Jackie is stunned

I found out in a letter once.
Jackie (*furiously*) How could you—never tell me!
Margaret It wouldn't have made any difference, Jackie.
Jackie You know it would! (*Angry tears*) Mummy—

A moment. Jackie can't speak

Suddenly Rosie bursts into the room with a sheet over her head

Rosie Whoo-oo-oo! I'm a ghost.
Jackie Oh—(*she drops the framed photo, which breaks*) Look what you made me do!
Rosie Sorry.
Margaret What on earth are you doing Rosie? Where's Mother?
Rosie We're folding sheets. The landing's a snow storm.
Margaret (*weary*) Oh dear. I'd better go and look. Jackie, you pick up the pieces.

Margaret exits

Rosie Never mind Jackie. (*She kisses her*) Look. Gran's cut holes for eyes in this sheet. She's done one for herself too, that'll give Mum a fright.
Jackie (*laughing*) Oh, Rosie . . .
Rosie What?
Jackie I don't know . . .
Rosie What's up?

Jackie fights tears. After a moment

Jackie Rosie, you must understand—(*Slight pause*) Mummy has—a lot to cope with.
Rosie Oh, she's been telling you about Dad, hasn't she?
Jackie What about Dad?
Rosie Don't sound so worried. Why d'you always think things are your fault, Jackie?
Jackie Does Mum work late?
Rosie Yeah. She's doing some new computer course in the evenings.
Jackie Does Dad mind?
Rosie Yeah, Mum drives him spare. They have rows a lot.
Jackie (*anxiously*) What about?
Rosie Oh I dunno, the washing or something. I just put my Walkman on.
Jackie Poor Mummy . . . why didn't she tell me about it?
Rosie Well she doesn't want you to know she's messed things up. C'mon, help me rip this sheet.
Jackie What for?

They rip the sheet in half

Rosie A banner. We're doing a Greenham protest outside the physics lab at school.

Jackie Why?

Rosie Secrecy kills. (*Pause*)—Nuclear secrecy. (*She holds out the half sheet*) Here, you can make one too.

Jackie (*holding up the sheet*) "Sorry Mummy."

Pause

Rosie How old are you?

Jackie Thirty. Why?

Rosie You should stop that sort of thing now, or you never will. You should hear Mum's "I'm sorry" voice on the phone to Gran.

Jackie Don't you worry about what Mummy thinks?

Rosie I worry about nuclear war, and not getting a job, and whether Mr Walsh the physics teacher fancies me. Mum doesn't understand.

Jackie Fancy not worrying.

Rosie He's old enough to be my Dad. Mega creepy. You're old enough to be my Mum! (*Pause*) I'm glad you're not.

Jackie Why?

Rosie Because it would be a mega pain having to live up to you. Grandad used to go on and on about you, you know.

Jackie He disapproved of me.

Rosie He didn't.

Jackie I'm not how he thinks a woman should be.

Rosie That's what he liked! You are dumb.

Jackie (*amazed*) It wasn't admiration you know, his will! It was revenge.

Rosie How?

Jackie I'd escaped. Families. Nearly. He's made me responsible for all of you now.

Pause

Rosie You are thick. He left you the money so you can open a gallery of your own.

Jackie (*as she takes this in*) What would you do with the money Grandad left?

Rosie I'd buy a baseball jacket instead of this yucky anorak Mum makes me wear. I wouldn't give it all to Mum and Gran, like you. I'd give some to Greenpeace. C'mon, let's go in the garden and practise our banners.

Rosie opens the french windows and runs out swirling the sheet like a flag

Jackie hesitates

Doris enters, carrying a half-filled bin liner

Doris There's some washing flapping in the garden.

Jackie It's Rosie. She wants to change the world. (*She pulls the french windows shut*)

Doris You used to be like that.

Jackie Have I changed so much?

Doris (*watching Rosie*) It was thick snow, that winter you came to say. After Margaret had taken Rosie. Not that you were in much of a state to enjoy Christmas.

Jackie You've still got my letter?

Doris Of course.

Jackie Rosie must have it the day she's sixteen.

Doris Oh you make me so angry, Jackie!—You have to ask for what you want.

Jackie Granny, I can't.

Doris You can.

Jackie But Mummy's got so much to—it's not a good time for her.

Doris There's always an excuse. (*Pause*) I never did ask for what I wanted. Resentment is a terrible thing, Jackie. You don't want to be resenting somebody at the end of your life.

Jackie (*avoiding this*) What's in the bin liner?

Doris (*stiffly*) The pale blue curtains from the bedroom.

Jackie Oh good. Pale blue's your favourite, isn't it?

Doris Jack chose all the colours in this house (*Slight pause*) Very artistic, visitors used to say. (*Pause*) Scarlet, I'll have in my new house (*Pause*)

Margaret enters carrying a bin liner. She puts it down

Margaret Everything in the bin liner is for Oxfam.

Doris Nothing ventured, Jackie.

Jackie Mummy ...

Margaret Jackie, if you're not doing anything, there's the spare room to sort out.

Jackie Yes, Mummy.

There is a rumbling noise beyond the hall

Doris I told you that boiler wasn't right, Margaret.

Margaret Yes Mother.

Margaret exits

Jackie (*picking up the bin liner with the blue curtains in it*) Shall I put these curtains with the stuff for Oxfam, Granny?

Doris There's something else in that bag, Jackie. Some things you left with me once.

Jackie What?

Doris The baby clothes.

Pause. Jackie can't cope with this

Jackie I'd better go and see if everything's all right in the kitchen.

Doris Are you going to give them away?

Jackie No. Thank you, for keeping them safe, Granny.

Jackie exits

Doris opens the french windows

Doris Rosie!

Rosie comes in laughing and breathless, with the banner

It's a waste of time. The world's going to end soon, I saw it on the television.

Rosie That's only the official view, you mustn't believe them . . . But it was scary when it blew up, wasn't it?

Margaret enters

Margaret What's blown up, Rosie dear?
Rosie The world.
Margaret Oh. That's all right. I thought it was something else.
Doris What?
Margaret Nothing, Mother.
Doris We thought perhaps the kitchen ceiling had come down. Jackie went to have a look. She's so good at that sort of thing.
Margaret (*wearily*) Yes Mother.

Margaret exits

Doris They work too hard.
Rosie You shouldn't wind them up.
Doris You should be helping them.
Rosie They'd only say I was more trouble.

They smile

Doris I'll show you something. (*She pulls the dustsheet off the piano*)

Pause

Rosie It's the piano.
Doris Don't you like it?
Rosie We've got a synth at school.
Doris I had a friend called Cynth.
Rosie What's this? (*She picks up a salver on top of the piano*)
Doris It's a salver. Jack's employees gave it him on his retirement. It's only plate, of course.
Rosie (*sniffing*) The silver smells funny. I hate old things.
Doris You hate dead things, not old things, Rosie. (*Pause*) So do I. (*Pause*) I'm old.
Rosie Hold this. So you can see your face in it.

Doris holds the salver

Sit down on the piano stool

Doris does so

Doris What are you going to do?
Rosie Aha. Close your eyes.

Rosie stands behind here and puts her hands on Doris's cheeks, gently pulling the skin back and taut

Smooth the wrinkles away . . .

Doris Nice warm hands, Rosie.

Rosie Now open your eyes, Gran.

Doris Oh! (*She studies her reflection*)

Rosie There, see. You're not old really. Only on the surface. (*A moment. Then lets go*) My outside's the same as inside. That's why when I talk Mum thinks I'm being rude.

Doris (*getting up and putting the salver in the box*) When you're old . . . if you're rude . . . they just think your mind is going., (*Pause*) They never understand that it's anger. (*Pause*) Help me polish the piano.

Rosie Do I have to?

Doris There's some dusters and polish in Margaret's holdall.

Rosie (*passing them; reading the tin*) "Bradley's Beeswax." With a picture of a bee. Here.

Doris That's Jack's firm, of course. (*She tries to unscrew the lid*) Can you unscrew it?

Rosie (*unscrewing the lid*) What was your surname, Gran?

Doris Partington. Here, you take this cloth, and do the legs.

Rosie does so

They polish the piano during the following

Rosie We're doing a project about you at school.

Doris About me?

Rosie Yeah, you're working-class Lancashire, aren't you?

Doris Do I look it?

Rosie Mmm . . . (*As if from a school book*) "Oldham families were all cotton or paper. Despite the decline in the manufacturing industries, community spirit remained strong."

Doris (*reminiscing*) You'd give a neighbour a bit of sugar, bit of soap, what they needed. When the King came, we scooped up the manure for the tomatoes. Pride costs nothing.

Rosie That's what they said on the documentary we saw at school.

Doris Did they now? You've missed a bit there, see. When Mother and I arrived in Jubilee Street, the landlady, a bit woman, arms like beef, though she wore fancy hats, said, "I didn't know you had a babby". "You never asked", said Mother. She did! And that was that.

Rosie You didn't have a dad?

Doris No.

Rosie Does Mum know?

Doris No.

Rosie Can it be our secret?

Doris If you like, Rosie. Of course people gossiped, but the girl next door was illegitimate too, it was more common than they put on those documentaries. I was instilled. To get on. Work hard and you will rise like bread, my mother said—Are you polishing that, or just resting your arm?—No one's ever told me what to do. Of course by the time I met Jack the neighbourhood wasn't what it used to be. Wicked things, even in

Oldham. Well, there was the Depression. When you've got no job you lose a sense of things. But we worked. We moved up. To Cheadle Hulme! (*Pause*) It was very—(*pause*)—snob. When Jack's parents came visiting I used to borrow the silver teapot from Next Door. Got in a fix one day, because Next Door's in-laws popped by the same afternoon. We had to pass it through the window, back and forth. (*Pause*) I never used bicarb, for my scones, just elbow. (*She rubs*) There now. We can see our faces in it.

Pause. They both admire it

It will fetch quite a bit I fancy.

Rosie You can sell pianos through the small ads.

Doris Jackie's organized an auction, hasn't she? Put these clothes away, they're soiled now.

Rosie opens Margaret's bin liner, thinking it's rubbish

That's not rubbish—

Rosie Hey it's full of clothes! (*She tips the bin liner all over the floor and picks some clothes up*) Cheesecloth and flares! Yuck. I didn't know you were a hippy once, Gran.

Doris Oh quite a—what's the word—"swinger".

Rosie No kidding?

Doris No. (*Pause*) Those were Jackie's—she came to stay with us once, left some things she didn't need any more.

Rosie Aren't they revolting! My big sister in these! (*She pulls out the ski pants Margaret wore in Act 1 Scene Seven*) Oh, can I have these ski pants?

Doris You can have what you like. Margaret obviously doesn't care for any of them. Everything's throwaway now, of course.

Rosie But these are brill Gran! Mega trendy.

Rosie pulls ski pants over her tights and skirt

Doris You don't want those slacks. There's a nice beige skirt here, see love. (*She picks out the skirt she wore in Act 1, Scene Seven*) Margaret bought those ... "pants" ... (*Disdainfully*) They're American.

Rosie Are they real fifties?

Doris There's generations here, all mixed up, if you poke about. (*She rummages in the bin liner*)

Margaret enters and goes to her holdall

Margaret Don't say I didn't bring rubber gloves ... (*She pulls a pair from her holdall and puts them on during the following*)

Rosie Mum, look!

Silence

D'you recognize them?

Silence

Gee, ah simply must do mah nails! (*She parades about*) Mum?

Margaret Rosie, we haven't time for dressing-up games.

Doris I think they rather suit her, Margaret.

Rosie They're really sexy. I can't imagine you fitting into these, Mum! Did she look nice in them, Gran?

Pause

Margaret Did I, Mother?

Pause

Rosie Can't you remember that far back?

Doris You only remember what you want.

Margaret Rosie, clear up this mess. We're going as soon as Jackie's fixed the boiler.

Margaret exits

Rosie I'm keeping these on for going home. Will you help me put my hair up, like they did?

Doris helps Rosie put her hair up

Doris A beehive? Sugar and water you need for that.

Rosie (*delighted*) Like a punk!

They stuff clothes back into the bin liner

(*Amused*)—Shall I keep this hippy stuff to show Jackie?

Doris I wouldn't bother.

Rosie Why not?—Really embarrass her!

Doris Not all memories are pleasant.

A Beat

Rosie We should hide some clothes in the cellar, for someone to find in a hundred years ...

Doris ties the bin liner shut. Rosie reaches for the other one

What's in here?

Doris Oh, Just some old curtains.

Rosie (*opening it*) What sweet little baby clothes! (*She tips them all over the floor*)—You're not looking, Gran!

Doris Put those back in the bag, Rosie.

Rosie I want this one with the little rabbits on.

Doris No. That belongs to Jackie.

Rosie I'll ask Jackie then.

Doris I should have known ...

Jackie enters distracted

Jackie Did I leave the stepladder in here? (*She stops, seeing the babyclothes everywhere*)

Rosie (*holding up the rabbit dress*) Look what I found!

Pause

Jackie Oh no please, not your rabbit dress.
Rosie Mine? Gran, you said this was Jackie's.
Doris Did I? Well, you ask Jackie.

Rosie looks at Jackie

Jackie (*slowly*) I bought it for you, Rosie.
Margaret (*calling from the hall*) Jackie!

Rosie whips the rabbit dress behind her just as:

   Margaret enters

Have you got that stepladder? (*She stops and takes in the scene*)
Rosie Guess what Mum, you'll never guess!
Margaret (*terrified*) What.
Rosie *Guess!* (*She brings out the rabbit dress from behind her back*) My baby
   dress! (*Pause*) And guess what Jackie told me—
Margaret (*giddy*) No . . .
Jackie It's OK everyone. Mummy it's OK.

She goes to Margaret but they can't hold each other

Rosie What?
Jackie Mummy's . . . not feeling well. Are you?
Margaret I'm perfectly all right!

Stasis

Doris I think I've had enough for today.
Jackie Yes, it's getting late, isn't it.
Rosie It's half past five, you wallies!
Margaret Rosie, don't shout.
Jackie Mummy, are you all right?
Doris I expect she's been overdoing it.
Margaret Rosie put those baby clothes in the bag for Oxfam.
Rosie Oh Mum, don't be *boring*.
Jackie Rosie! She's just sitting down.
Rosie *I can see she's sitting down!*
Doris You're tired, dear.
Rosie I'm *not tired!*
Jackie You are!
Rosie Not you too!
Doris Margaret, have you seen my piano?
Margaret It's over there, Mother.
Doris I *know*. I'm talking about the polish. You've not even noticed, have
   you?
Margaret Oh *Mother*! What did you do that for? It'll only need polishing
   again after the move.
Doris I'm selling it. At the auction.
Margaret But it's the only thing Father left for you.

Doris It was mine anyway. I bought it with my savings from teaching, when I got married. (*Pause*) You never knew, did you?

Margaret You can't ...

Rosie 'Course she can.

Jackie Food; everyone into the car.

Rosie I'm not hungry yet.

Margaret Mother needs to have her tea promptly, don't you dear?

Doris Oh I'm no trouble. I shall have a boiled egg.

Rosie Can we got to MacDonald's? Yeah!

Jackie We're all going to my flat.

Margaret You don't cook, Jackie.

Jackie We're getting a take-out Indian. There's a good place on the Stockport Road.

Margaret Mother can't possibly chew spare ribs.

Doris Chew what?

Rosie I hate curry. I want a Macdonalds. Can I keep these on?

Doris Yes.

Margaret No. Have you got your handbag, Mother?

Doris I don't need helping, thank you. Are you going home in rubber gloves?

Jackie Mummy, are you OK to drive, if I take the van?

Margaret (*picking up the Thermos and Thermos cup*) Does anyone want this tea ... ?

Rosie Mu-um, it's cold. Knowing you, you'll probably take it home and save it for tomorrow.

Margaret Rosie! (*She tips the tea into the Thermos and screws the cup on*)

Jackie I'll take these out to the van. (*She goes to the bin liners. She sees a dress lying behind them*) What's this dress? I didn't see it before—it looks like an original 1920s!

Doris I think there was a tea stain ... no, it was a grass stain ... I wore that frock the day that Jack proposed.

Jackie hesitates, holding up the dress. No response. She puts it in the bin liner and ties it shut

Margaret I'm going to check the windows and turn the power off. You two get in the car.

Margaret exits

Jackie I'll see you both back at my flat. (*She hesitates*) Look at you with your hair up like that, Rosie! I wish you were still a baby. You were so sweet ...

Rosie Was I?

Doris There was a time for babies, Jackie, and it's gone.

Rosie Ow, Jackie you always hug too hard!

Doris Truth will out, Jackie. Don't say I didn't warn you.

Rosie C'mon Gran, let's go.

Jackie looks at Doris, picks up the bin liners and goes

Doris Come along Rosie, put your anorak on.

As Doris helps Rosie into her anorak, the room is suddenly plunged into darkness

Oh!

Rosie I left the big torch on the landing!—Wait there, Gran.

Rosie exits

Doris goes to the french windows

The sound of wind

Jack? Jack ... You should see how the roses have all blown down in the garden ... crushed ... You rattle like a dry pod, now. Skin on your skull like frayed paper (*Pause*) I tried so hard, even in those last few years ... Something nourishing and not difficult to chew ... The tray pushed aside on your bed. You did that deliberately, didn't you?

The wind rattles the windows

When you died and the nurses left me alone with you, to pray I suppose, I climbed into bed beside you, yes I did, lay beside you then ... the sun was shining through the window, hot; only you were cold as ice.

Rosie enters, carrying a round wooden board and the flashlight. She swings the flashlight around the room until the beam comes to rest on Doris's face. Doris has been crying

Rosie —Gran?
Doris Give me a minute. I'll put my hat and gloves on.
Rosie Gran? Hurry, what are you doing?

A car horn honks outside

Doris Are they waiting for us?
Rosie (*gently*) You haven't got any gloves ... Oh Gran. (*She goes to Doris. A split second of hesitation*)
Doris Don't kiss—
Rosie Yes!

Rosie kisses Doris. Doris strokes Rosie's hair

Doris Lovely hair ... mine are all old grey hairs ...
Rosie (*holds up the wooden board*) Look, Gran, look what I found in the spare room. What is it?
Doris Solitaire. Why, that was my mother's, she gave it me. It's a game. I used to sit and play it in the evenings, while Jack read the papers. You have to get rid of all the marbles from the holes in the board, until there is just one left, in the centre. Solitaire.

The car horn sounds again

Rosie Can we take it with us?
Doris Yes, if you want, Rosie.

Rosie Will you show me how to do it?
Doris If you come and visit me. Put your hood up now, it's snowing out.

Rosie takes the Solitaire board and flashlight. She swings the beam round the room one last time

They exit

The sound of car doors slamming outside, and then the car and van driving off in the snow

The sound of wind and snow blizzard around the house becomes louder

Black-out

ACT III

The backyard of Doris's terrace house in Oldham, early April 1987

Doris is eighty-seven and wears a floral overall; Margaret is fifty-six, dressed in the sensible suit she wears to work, wearing an apron she has borrowed from Doris. They are chatting as they come out of the back kitchen door. Margaret carrying a tray of small geraniums in pots, Doris carrying a tray and kneeler. They kneel beside a tub and a bag of potting compost

Doris See dear, all those are from the one plant I brought with me from Cheadle Hulme.

Margaret I've had mine in the kitchen all winter, but they've not done so well.

Doris Oh you have to cut them right down until they're just dry sticks, then all of a sudden, it seems, they start producing new leaves.

Margaret They'll look lovely in this tub.

Doris I've had a postcard from Rosie. She and Jackie seem to be having a lovely time.

Margaret Yes. It's very quiet at home.

Pause

Margaret continues planting a geranium in the tub

Doris You look thinner. Are you eating properly?

Margaret What do you mean?

Doris Don't crowd the roots—Well—you coming all the way from London like this—on a Tuesday!

Margaret Can't I even come and see you for the day without—

Doris Usually you're so busy, at that office . . . never have time to come and visit.

Margaret Yes, well I took the day off!

Doris No need to snap, dear.

Pause

Margaret digs a hole

Margaret You've transformed this backyard. I must say.

Doris Yes, I'm quite proud, it's only five years since the move. Cheadle Hulme will be a mass of blossom, now, of course. The jasmine hasn't done very well, but then it's been such a spring.

Margaret Good (*Pause*) I mean, sorry, yes, it's been awful, spring, hasn't it.

Doris How are your geranium tubs doing?

Margaret Mmm.

Doris I ate my shoe this afternoon.

Margaret Yes. (*She picks a leaf and stares at it*)

Doris Margaret, you're not listening to a word I'm saying, are you?

Margaret Of course ...

Doris What's wrong, Margaret?

Margaret What do you mean, what's wrong?

Doris You're upset.

Margaret I'm probably upset because you're accusing me of being upset.

Doris (*smoothly*) I'm not accusing you. Don't take umbrage.

Margaret Really, Mother. I make the effort to come here for a friendly visit and you react as though there's something wrong! Can't I even have a normal conversation with my own mother?

Doris I don't know, dear.

Margaret What do you mean, you don't know? (*Pause*) And don't call me "dear"!

Doris Trains from London are so expensive at this time of day.

Margaret There, see? We can't even talk without the housekeeping coming into it.

Pause

Doris (*gently*) What is it, dear? It's Ken, isn't it?

Silence

He's not been made redundant?

Silence

Margaret I don't know.

Doris What do you mean, you don't know.

Margaret I haven't seen Ken for a week, Mother. (*Pause*) I don't think it's another woman. He's not like that. And we've always been very happy. I know it happens to one in three marriages these days, but—you don't think of yourself as a statistic, do you? (*Pause*) Mummy, I still want him.

Doris Your Father ... stopped "wanting me", many years ago. One didn't divorce, then. I thought if I persisted in loving him ... I wanted to—to be desired. (*Pause*) The night he died, we embraced. He held my hand; he said he loved me most that night. I believed him ... Was it worth it, I ask myself? (*Silence*) You've made more of your life. A job and that.

Margaret Exactly. It's all my fault. He loved me, Mother ... but he didn't want to share me.

Doris With who?

Margaret With the job. Trying to work and look after Rosie ... Well I had to work, London's so expensive now. (*Pause*) But Ken married a wife, not a working mother.

Doris You expected too much. So did I. And Jackie expects even more. (*Pause*) My father turned up once, after we'd moved to Jubilee Street. Mother took him back, of course. I saw the marks, when she was bathing in front of the fire. She said it was because he loved her so much, he hugged her too tight. (*Pause*) When I think about Jack. I think, well I was lucky really.

Doris gently lowers the geranium plant into the hole Margaret has dug. Margaret pats soil around it

Come in the cottage with me, dear. There's something I want to give you. (*Pause*) You've never seen a photograph of my mother, have you?
Margaret (*a white lie*) No.

Margaret stands, and helps Doris stand. They brush the earth from their aprons

   They go in together

SCENE 2

Croydon, London, early April 1987, four days later

A bright sunny morning in Margaret's office, but there is traffic noise outside. A desk, a telephone, a typewriter, a pot of geraniums and a photo frame. Margaret is fifty-six, Jackie is thirty-four, Rosie is fifteen and a half

Margaret is seated, uncovering the typewriter. She wears a sensible suit as in the previous scene

Rosie enters with an orange kite and a bundle of letters, which she puts on Margaret's desk. She wears chic holiday clothes

Rosie Morning post, Mrs Metcalfe.
Margaret Rosie! What on earth are you doing here?

Rosie kisses Margaret then makes the kite swoop round the office space

Rosie Look, isn't it beautiful!
Margaret Have you been home yet?
Rosie No. We came straight from the airport, all the way in a taxi, can you imagine! But Jackie says when it's important you have to do these things.
Margaret (*touching her hair*) Is she here too?
Rosie Yes. Only she's gone in the third floor Ladies to change into her Art Dealer dress. She doesn't want you to see her looking a mess.
Margaret Is she going straight back to work?
Rosie There's some meeting about the future of her gallery, with the Manchester City Council. (*She swoops the kite*)
Margaret But you've both been travelling all night.
Rosie So?
Margaret You'd better get out of sight before Mr Reece arrives at nine.
Rosie Don't you like it? Such style, the Italians.
Margaret How was Venice?

Rosie Brilliant! "Fettucine alla casa, va bene?"! The food was marvellous. Dad would have hated it!

Margaret I'm sure.

Rosie I can't believe it's only a week! What have you been up to? You didn't clean my room?

Margaret I went to visit Granny.

Rosie I sent her a postcard of the beach where we flew this kite. Also we brought some Chianti back for Dad, and you'll never guess what we've brought you! Did Dad water my tomatoes?

Pause

Margaret (*pause*) Dad's been away for the week. What did you like best in Venice?

Rosie Oh, definitely the carnival. We stayed up all night, everyone wore masks like birds, that's when I saw the kites. We had breakfast at San Marco's, and this man fell in love with Jackie, so I just stared into the canal and ordered another cappuccino, and pretended I was waiting for a gondola. And then it turned out it was me he fancied, and Jackie got very cross with him in Italian, and we had to leave.

Margaret I hope you didn't stay up every night?

Rosie Oh yes—Mum, of course not. I mean—Jackie's so sweet, she was trying so hard to be like you.

Margaret Like me?

Rosie Yes. I can't think of anyone less like a mother (*Pause*) You know Mum, sometimes you have to be a bit silly with Jackie just to get her to relax. She needs . . .

Margaret What does she need?

Rosie . . . I don't know . . . it's hard to explain. (*She thinks*) She's so restless: she's always looking for something to do. We spent a whole day trekking round museums but she could never find the picture she wanted. After I'd got this kite, we went to this incredibly long beach, ran for miles. (*She swoops the kite*) We were shouting because of the wind, and Jackie got the kite to do a perfect circle in the sky . . . Oh Mum, it was such a brilliant day . . . Will you stop opening letters for a minute—

Margaret I am at work.

Rosie Yes, but I have to tell you something! Oh Mum, it's incredible!

Margaret What, dear?

Rosie Well, I asked Jackie—I couldn't believe she'd agree—I want to go and live with her in Manchester!

A long pause

Margaret What about your exams?

Rosie Oh, I won't go till the summer, of course. Anyway, Jackie says we have to discuss it with you and Dad first. (*Pause*) Mum . . . ?

Margaret You've no idea. Jackie can't cook, she'll forget to wash your clothes . . .

Rosie I know! She's so useless at most things. Not like you. (*Pause*) She needs me. (*Pause*) I'll come back and visit, lots.

Margaret Whenever you can afford the fare.

Rosie Oh Jackie will pay. She says we'll both visit. She comes to London all the time, anyway.

Margaret Does she?

Rosie (*cutting in*) You said! Don't you remember? You promised, after my exams I could do whatever I wanted.

A long pause

Margaret Yes, I did. (*She turns away, afraid she's going to cry*) I've got to ... write a letter, Rosie, can you wait outside a minute ...

Rosie exits, swooping the kite as she goes

Jackie and Rosie meet in the corridor. Jackie is wearing a flowery dress, carrying a Chinese lacquered briefcase and a blue kite

Rosie Don't go in. (*She surveys Jackie*) You've spoiled it now. Miss Executive. You should got to work wearing that turquoise thing.

Jackie That was a beach dress.

Rosie Suited you much better.

Jackie It's an incredibly important meeting.

Rosie All the more reason to let them see what you're really like.

Jackie I can't start now.

Rosie You could. If you wanted. Come outside and fly this kite with me.

Jackie I want to see Mummy.

Rosie She's busy.

Jackie I'll sit in her office and prepare for my meeting.

Rosie See—now you're being all business woman again!

Jackie Calm down. You're not at home now.

Rosie Mum isn't like you when she's at work. (*She goes, swooping the kite*)

Jackie (*entering the office*) Mum! I'm sorry. Didn't you get the message? The delay was twelve hours in the end, airport like an oven.

Margaret Rosie's hopelessly over-excited.

Jackie I know Mummy, I couldn't get her to sleep. But she's been so good all week, you don't need to worry. She's very sensible for fifteen. Wouldn't let me swim too far out.

Margaret She'll be tired for the first day of term now.

Jackie That's three days away!

Margaret There's all her clothes to wash.

Jackie I'd do it, but I've ...

Margaret Got to go back to Manchester for a meeting.

Pause

Jackie (*pause*) Rosie can wash her own things. She did all our clothes one evening, fixed up a line on the balcony.

Margaret It's an adventure with you. (*Pause*) You should see her bedroom, it's like a junkyard—clothes, glue, paint.

Jackie She's very creative. Kept writing poetry in the restaurant.

Margaret (*testing Jackie*) She's full of crazy ideas.

Jackie (*pause; cautiously*) Is she?

No reply from Margaret

It's just her energy, isn't it?

Margaret Well of course with you ...

Jackie She talks about you a lot.

Margaret What about?

Jackie Oh, I only mean your job. She wanted to show me all round where you work.

Margaret Did she?

Jackie You didn't tell me you were promoted last year. (*She looks over Margaret's shoulder at the letters she is opening*)

Margaret It's nothing glamorous.

Jackie You know I'd be useless at this. My typing's awful ... Do you have to reply to all these?

Margaret Mr Reece dictates, I spend the rest of the morning unravelling his grammar, otherwise British Microwaves would never have any exportable trade. These young graduates.

Jackie I hope they pay you the right scale. You're the one who does all the work.

Margaret I'm only his personal assistant.

Jackie Don't say "only".

Margaret Oh I was lucky. My typing speeds are very ordinary. It's only that I've got Pitman's Classic and most of the girls don't learn shorthand these days.

Jackie I'm sure it's other qualities got you this job, Mummy.

Pause

Margaret (*pleased*) It's funny, hearing "Mummy" in this place. You do a job, people treat you differently.

Jackie It's only how you treat yourself.

Pause

Margaret You look radiant, dear.

Jackie Swimming and sea air. (*Quietly*) Bit of sun, Mummy. Do you good, too.

Margaret (*quietly*) Sat in the garden this weekend. Been very ... Been a relief, you having Rosie for this week.

Pause

Jackie I hope you kept the appointment? She's a nice woman, isn't she?

Margaret It was a very expensive-looking waiting room.

Jackie Mummy, I asked you to see the specialist, not the wallpaper. What did she say?

Margaret Oh—nothing much.

Jackie Did she do some tests?

Margaret No.

Jackie No?

Margaret Says I'm fine. Just menopause, probably.

Pause

Jackie Honestly?

Pause

Margaret What do you mean?

Jackie Well—(*Pause*)—That's such a relief! (*She laughs*) Oh Mummy. We even got a taxi all the way here!

Pause

Margaret Now you can go and catch your train to Manchester, can't you?

Jackie Mum . . . May Bank holiday, come and stay with me. Just you, and we'll . . .

Margaret Fly kites.

Jackie (*laughing, holding out the kite*) Oh yes, Rosie and I bought you a kite. She says Daddy will show you how to fly it, but I said you're an expert. Do you remember, how you took me flying kites in Richmond Park, and once it got stuck in a chestnut tree, and all the conkers came down?

Margaret I thought you'd wiped out that little girl.

Jackie So did I. Rosie won't. She'll have kites in her office, or whatever. (*Pause*) I used to wear suits, when I first started my job. (*She puts the kite on the desk and knocks the photo frame off the desk*) Oh sorry (*She bends and picks up the photo frame*) Is this Cornwall?—Rosie . . . Oh isn't she sweet! Can I have a copy of this one?

Pause

Margaret Rosie's told me, Jackie.

Jackie (*terrified*) I wasn't going to—

Margaret No, I expect you had another date planned when you were going to tell me that you'd like Rosie back. Or perhaps you were just going to tell me over the phone.

Jackie You need time, to decide . . . in the summer.

Margaret It's not my decision. It's Rosie's. And she's made her mind up. (*Pause*) I knew she'd say it one day. Like one of those fairy-tales.

Jackie You haven't told her!

Margaret Of course not. She still thinks you're big sister, that's why it's so magical to her.

Jackie We were running along this dazzling beach. I thought, is that what I've missed?

Margaret Years and years and years you've lost, Jackie. Birthdays and first snowman and learning to ride a bicycle and new front teeth. You can't pull them back.

Jackie I can make up for it—somehow—

Margaret You can't. Those are my years.

Jackie She must remember—I visited!

Margaret Treats, she's had with you. A day here and there. That never fooled her. But I let it fool you. I'm the woman who sat up all night with the sick child, who didn't mind all her best crockery getting broken over the years.

Jackie Mummy ...

A long pause

Margaret (*coolly*) What time's your train?

Jackie Nine forty-five—no—I could get the ten forty-five.

Margaret You mustn't miss your meeting.

Jackie It would give us another hour. I wish we weren't in your office! (*She panics*) Where's Rosie gone?

Margaret Are you going to catch that train, or stay here? You can't do both.

Pause. Jackie agonizes

I'll phone you a taxi. (*She dials, waits; the line is engaged*)

Jackie (*quietly*) You know Mum, the gallery and everything, I couldn't have done it without you. You can't be a mother and then cancel Christmas to be in New York.

The telephone connects

Margaret (*on the phone*) Taxi to Euston please, immediately. British Microwaves, front entrance. (*She puts the receiver down*)

Jackie Come and stay, show me how you do things, how Rosie would like her room decorated.

Margaret No Jackie, I shall just put a label around Rosie's neck, and send her Red Star. (*She doesn't look at Jackie any more but busies herself with papers*) It's gone nine. I wonder where Mr Reece is?

Jackie runs out of the room

Margaret bursts into tears

The telephone rings

(*Picking up the receiver*) Hello? Hello. yes, I'll be with you directly. (*She puts down the receiver*) Oh God, my mascara—all over the letters. (*She dabs her eyes and the letters*) Every day, getting up at six to make Rosie's picnic lunch and Ken's supper for the oven. It will be strange to be a single woman again. (*Pause. She is calm now*) I'll oversleep. I'll go and fly my kite, in Richmond Park. (*She gets up to go out of the office, turns back to the telephone, dials*) Hello? Is that Manchester City Art Gallery? Yes, I'd like to leave a message for Jackie Metcalfe, just say—(*Pause*)—May Bank Holiday will be fine. (*She puts the phone down*)

Margaret walks out of the office

Black-out

SCENE 3

The wasteground

Cats wail

It is almost dark. We see the glint of faces and hands

Jackie Hare lip and eye of bat.
Rosie Poisoned dewdrop and tail of cat.
Jackie Put it in a monkey's hat.
Doris What's a monkey's hat?
Jackie Ssh!
Rosie You can't have hare lip.
Jackie Sssh!
Doris Why?
Rosie It's something real. You get it. I've seen a lady with it in the opticians.
Doris What's it like?
Jackie (*She stirs twig potage*) Sssh! I can't concentrate. This is a laboratory.
Rosie It's a sort of slit in your mouth, goes up your nose.
Doris Eugh.
Rosie You're born with it. It means you're missing a bit in the head, too.
Jackie Shut up!
Doris Let's go and have a look!
Rosie Optician's closed.
Jackie (*mysteriously*) She didn't used to have it. It grew.
Rosie Honest?
Jackie Maybe *we* did it. (*Pause*)
Rosie How could we ...
Doris Could we?
Jackie (*grandly*) I can tell you what her name is.
Rosie Go on.
Jackie Mrs Worsley.
Doris 'S right!
Jackie See? Proves it. Our powers.
Doris What powers?
Jackie In the earth.
Rosie What happens to people when they die, then?
Jackie They rot. Worms go in their nose and out their eyeballs.
Doris No! (*She starts to cry*) I don't want to do that—
Jackie It's too late.

The shadowy figure of Margaret appears upstage and starts walking towards them

Rosie I don't want to do that to Mum!
Jackie 'S too late. Was her idea.
Doris No.
Rosie No it wasn't, it was yours.
Doris Stop it!
Rosie Stop the spell.

Doris Make it go backwards!
Jackie You can't make someone's life go backwards.
Rosie I'm going to tell her—c'mon!
Doris (*as she goes*) Wasn't me!

Rosie grabs Doris and they run off

Jackie She'll be dead when you get there.

Cats wail

I didn't mean to do it! Don't leave me all alone!

Jackie runs off

SCENE 4

Margaret enters in a hospital gown, with her hair scraped back. Her face is drawn, and very white. Late May 1987. Under anaesthetic

Margaret (*wandering*) I know the door is here somewhere, if only I could find it, the door to the garden ... Here's a door ... the bathroom! ... What a cold wind blowing through here ... Why, here we are, on its iron legs, the white enamel bath ... cold on your bare flesh, even in summer ... goosepimples ... Father's made his fortune! But we still have to save hot water ... Everything is a sacrifice in this house. Everything—is—sacrifice—for ... Private tennis lessons. Piano tuition. Tu-ition.... BUT! (*She whispers conspiratorially*) One must go to the bathroom and lock the door if one wants—needs—to (*She shouts*) CRY! ... When you pull the plug out, the water gets sucked down with a roar ... GrrOWrr ... So they know I'm here ... is no privacy in this huge house ... My parents are called, my parents are called ... Guilt, and ... Duty. Wonderful, how they keep the family together ... we were semi-detached, now we're detached ... When *I* have babies, they will be called ... Sugar—and Spice— ... and all things nice ... I will give them everything they want, and they will love me ... Mother? ... Mummy ... What happens when you die? ... I wish they wouldn't keep opening the door, it's so cold ... I'm sure I can find the garden, if I just keep going.

The lights fade on her. We hear a baby crying, after a moment a child joins in crying

Fade out

SCENE 5

The garden of Ken and Margaret's suburban semi in Rayne's Park, London. It is late May 1987, early morning, two hours after Scene Four

Rosie sits on the swing beneath the cherry tree with the old red transistor

Jackie runs across the garden, hot and grubby, carrying her lacquered briefcase

LBC Radio ... more congestion on the North Circular. Meanwhile the overturned tanker is still blocking the Blackwall Tunnel. And it's coming up to eight o'clock, a lovely May morning ... Looking down the Euston Road, here's to the girl in that blue Mini, a thought from the Beatles ... (*Music: "All You Need Is Love"*)

Jackie Rosie? ...

Silence. Hold this for as long as possible while Jackie has to cope with it

Rosie I hope you're a success, Jackie. A big, big success.

Jackie Rosie are you all right? Where's Daddy?

Rosie I hope lots of people came to your opening and thought your gallery was brill.

Jackie It was only twelve hours—I'd never have gone back to Manchester if I'd thought—after Daddy phoned, last night, there were no more planes, I got the first plane I could this morning.

Rosie In case you want to know, she died at 6.20 last night. Dad was with her. They said it was quicker at the end. It wasn't just stomach cancer, there were secondaries.

Jackie (*goes to hug Rosie who won't let her*) If only I'd been here with you ...

Rosie (*turns away*) Did you sell lots of your paintings?

Jackie Rosie—

Rosie Did you?

Jackie I didn't sell any. I cancelled the opening.

Rosie I don't believe you. You'd never do that.

Silence

Jackie What do we do ... now? ... I'll call a taxi to the hospital—do we have to take things—her birth certificate? ... I don't know ...

Rosie Dad's done all that. He's been brilliant, like it was before they split up. He knew where Mum kept the box that's got all the family stuff in it. Look—he said I could have this one—(*She holds out a photo*) That's Mum holding me by the front door when I'd just arrived ... And ... (*She lays them on the grass*)—Here's Mum's birth certificate, ... and here's mine.

Silence

Jackie No.

Rosie So now I know.

Jackie (*desperately*) I was going to tell you—in five months—when you were sixteen ... Mummy said to wait till after your exams, so as not to upset you ...

Rosie has a handful of photos and throws them down one by one ... except for one which she slips in her pocket

Rosie Nineteen seventy-two, my first birthday, nineteen seventy-three, my second birthday, Christmas nineteen seventy-five, nineteen seventy-six;

then you were in South America, nineteen seventy-nine with the birthday cake, nineteen eighty-two when we cleared Gran and Grandad's house—and our week in Venice. (*Pause*) Have them. Have them all.

Jackie Rosie—we've got to help each other now.

Rosie Why don't you go and get drunk, or whatever it is you lot do to show you're feeling something.

Pause

Jackie I wanted you to have opportunities I couldn't ever have given you.

Rosie No, you didn't. You wanted your own life more than you wanted mine!

Jackie Don't!

Rosie If you were really my mum you wouldn't have been able to give me away!

Jackie How dare you! (*She goes to hit Rosie but cannot*) You're at the centre of everything I do! (*A slight pause*) Mummy treated me as though I'd simply fallen over and cut my knee,—picked me up and said you'll be all right now, it won't show much. She wanted to make it all better. (*Quietly*) . . . She was the one who wanted it kept secret . . . I WANTED you, Rosie. (*Angrily*) For the first time in my life I took care of myself—refused joints, did exercises, went to clinic. (*Pause*) "It's a girl". (*She smiles irresistibly*)— After you'd gone I tried to lose that memory. (*Pause. With effort*) Graham . . . your father. (*Silence*) He couldn't be there the day you were born, he had to be in Liverpool. He was married. (*Emphatically*) He loved me, he loved you, you must believe that! (*Pause*) He said he'd leave his wife, but I knew he wouldn't; there were two children, the youngest was only four . . . we'd agreed, separate lives. I wanted to bring you up. He sent money. (*Pause*) I took you to Lyme Park one day, I saw them together, across the lake, he was buying ice creams, his wife was taking a photo. I think they live in Leeds now, I saw his name in the *Guardian* last year, an article about his photographs . . . (*Pause*) It was a very cold winter after you were born. There were power cuts. I couldn't keep the room warm; there were no lights in the tower blocks; I knew he had an open fire, it was trendy; so we took a bus to Didsbury, big gardens, pine kitchens, made a change from concrete. I rang the bell. (*She stops*) A Punjabi man answered, said he was sorry . . . they'd moved. By the time we got back to Hulme it was dark, the lift wasn't working—(*She stops*) That was the night I phoned Mummy. (*With difficulty*) Asked her. (*Pause*) I tried! I couldn't do it, Rosie. (*Pause*) It doesn't matter how much you succeed afterwards, if you've failed once. (*Pause*) After you'd gone . . . I kept waking in the night to feed you . . . A week . . . in the flat . . . Then I went back to art school. Sandra and Hugh thought I was inhuman. I remember the books that came out that winter—how to succeed as a single working mother—fairy-tales! (*Pause*) Sandra and Hugh have a family now. Quite a few of my friends do. (*Pause*) I could give you everything now. Rosie? . . .

Pause

Rosie I used to hate you, only I never knew why. (*She gestures*) Sit down on the swing. I'm going to Oldham, to live with Gran—Great-Gran. Dad says I can.

Jackie hesitates

Jackie I'm frightened.

Rosie Put your head back and look up through the cherry tree. The sky is falling. Mum used to sit here with me in her arms, and I'd pretend I was asleep. (*She gets up*) I'm never having any children. (*She starts towards the house*)

Jackie You might.

Rosie hears, but keeps walking away

The lights fade to black-out

SCENE 6

(*This scene was cut for the Royal Court production*)

The wasteground, Oldham. Idyllic sunshine

Margaret walks in, balancing on cracks of paving

Margaret King of the Golden River! (*She demonstrates an invisible line*) I'm the King.

Jackie runs in

Jackie Farmer Farmer, may I cross your golden river, just to take our Daddy's dinner.

Jackie runs to cross the line, Margaret chases and catches her

Margaret You've got to do a dare ...!
Jackie I've been in the boys' den ...
Margaret And?
Jackie They wanted me to kill you.
Margaret It didn't work.
Jackie Sure?
Margaret Yes.

Slight pause

Jackie The others won't play with me any more.
Margaret Tell you what.
Jackie What?
Margaret You can come with me. To my secret, secret hide.

Margaret holds out her hand. Margaret and Jackie run off together as the lights fade

SCENE 7

Oldham, September 1987. The backyard of Doris's end terrace cottage

There are two deckchairs; the piano stool from Acts I and II, on it the Solitaire board from Act II; a tub of geraniums; a yellow kite

Rosie is sunbathing in cut-off jeans and painted T-shirt, both of which she has tie-dyed herself, wearing Walkman headphones, oblivious of all other noise. She hums "Holding Back The Years", as she concentrates on the Solitaire game

A moment. The distant sound of children playing

Doris appears upstage, holding up the kite's tail

Doris (*calling*) Is this right?

Rosie continues humming. Doris comes nearer

Rosie? CAN YOU HEAR ME, DEAR? (*She taps Rosie on the shoulder*)
Rosie SORRY! (*She removes the headphones*)
Doris You're shouting again dear. Neighbours will think I'm deaf. (*She holds up the kite tail*) Is this right?
Rosie Looks great! Thanks. (*She picks up the kite*) Here, just tie it on the bottom.

Doris ties the kite tail to the kite

Doris Needs a stitch in it.
Rosie (*holding the kite aloft*) What d'you think?

Pause

Doris I preferred the blue ones.
Rosie Well they've ordered fifty, so I'm not complaining. (*She puts the kite down*) Did ten this morning.
Doris I gathered that, from the state of the box room. Bits of string ...
Rosie It's not for you to clear up. Sit down Doris, enjoy the sun.
Doris (*sitting*) I fancy one of those garden tables ... white ones, with an umbrella. But they do cost, don't they?
Rosie (*firmly*) When I've sold the next batch, maybe. We mustn't spend before we've paid off the overheads.
Doris You shouldn't be bothering your head with work on your birthday. (*Pause*) Just like your mother.
Rosie Did you see her present!
Doris Mrs W saw me take it in. Postman couldn't get it through the letterbox.
Rosie It's one of her paintings.
Doris I propped it on the mantelpiece.
Rosie What d'you think?

Pause

Doris I liked the gold frame. Looks expensive.
Rosie Gran! She did it specially for me.

A lull. Rosie returns to the Solitaire

You promised to show me how to solve the Solitaire, today.
Doris You work it out. (*She watches Rosie for a moment*) No cheating,
mind. Took my mother years to work it out. She showed me, but she
made me vow never to tell anyone. I didn't even tell Jack, and husbands
and wives aren't supposed to have any secrets, are they?
Rosie Listen, I've been trying all week, and I can't do it.
Doris One week is nothing.

Rosie studies the board

Isn't this sunshine cheering? (*She puts on a pair of mirrored sunglasses*)
Rosie What do you think my next move should be?
Doris What do you think, Rosie?
Rosie (*laughing*) Oh Doris, take my shades off!
Doris They're mine. Bought them at the checkout when I went for the ice
cream.
Rosie There's a new Pakistani shop opened. Even cheaper than Kwiksave.
Doris Jack came home one night and I was sat in the dark. I told him, I'm
economising. He said, that's just as well, you left the hall light on. (*Pause*)
You can't win.
Rosie You can. Look, double jump! Is that allowed?
Doris Yes. Do you know, I think I'll even take my stockings off, and then
my legs can brown. (*She modestly reaches under her skirt and unhooks her
stockings*) Well, I may be as old as the Queen Mother, but *I* buy all my
smalls in Top Shop.
Rosie Hmmm . . . (*She removes another marble*)
Doris Do you know, Rosie, there's no such snob as the snob who rises from
the gutter . . .
Rosie Are you casting aspersions again? Grubbing at the Royal Family this
time, are you?
Doris No. As a matter of fact I was making an inference to my late
husband. Jack would never have tolerated this lack of modesty in a
woman (*Pause*) Although while we're on the subject, it is true that the
Queen Mother was a commoner before she married up.
Rosie AH! Triple jump! Fucking brill!
Doris Does one have to lower the tone of the afternoon quite so crudely?
Rosie Stop attempting posh, Doris. Your slip is showing.
Doris Is it? . . . Still, I don't suppose the Queen Mother does all her own
washing . . . (*She leans back and closes her eyes*)

Rosie puts the headphones back on. She hums

A lull

I suppose now you've got hold of that game, I won't be hearing from you
till the Christmas after next.

Rosie (*singing softly; moving a marble*) Ah!

Doris (*opening her eyes*) What with that electronic earmuff you wear, night and day.

Rosie (*studying the board*) Hmm ...

Doris In my day, families practised the art of conversation.

Rosie Aah! (*She removes another marble*)

Doris (*watching Rosie fondly*) Your mother couldn't solve that. Though she tried.

Rosie (*removing the headphones*) Are you talking to me? (*She stretches*) Mmm! It's hot, like being inside a blue balloon. (*She gazes out*) The moors are clear today. We should've walked up to the Waterloo Memorial.

Doris (*gazing out*) Wicked, sticking these tower blocks in the view.

Rosie It's so lovely here, Doris. (*Pause*) Ken phoned to say happy birthday. I asked him to put some special flowers on Margaret's grave today.

Pause

Doris To think, Jack and I in this same street sixty years ago—scrimping and saving so that our child would have a better start in life ... You do what you believe is best for your daughter, you know Rosie, and then you find it wasn't what she wanted. Or needed.

Rosie Remember what Jackie said afterwards. We mustn't live in the past.

Doris Well I don't see that I've much of a future with you. Stuck here with my great-granddaughter in a two-up, two-down.

Rosie Gran!

Doris (*winding her up*) Sat here forced to do piecework, tying scraps of coloured paper to lengths of string all day long ...

Rosie How much do you want that garden table ... ?

Doris You fancy you can bribe your great-grandmother?

Rosie Yes.

Pause

Doris How many did you say you wanted?

Rosie Fifty. By the end of the week. We can do them sitting out here.

Doris "Campaign Kites" ... Who'd have thought you'd earn a living off them.

Rosie moves another marble

Who are they for this time?

Rosie Greenpeace.

Doris Had another phone call from that Animal Liberation man.

Rosie I won't do business with organizations that use violence. (*Pause*) What did you tell him?

Doris That he was politically unsound.

Rosie That's a good phrase.

Doris Heard a girl say it at the evening class.

Rosie Let me guess ... Tricia?

Doris No—a new girl in Women's Literature. She's from the tower block over there. I've met her in the Welfare with her two babbies, and do you know, she doesn't look the sort to even open a book. But she's quite the best, the comments she comes out with in class. She can't spell, of course. (*Pause*) But it just goes to show: you can't judge by appearances. Jack was wrong (*Pause*) Even so, I do wish you wouldn't wear those dirty rags. You look ... like a victim.

Rosie I made this T-shirt for remembrance. It's like the Waterloo Memorial. It got ripped at the last march. Perhaps someone will find it in our cellar one day, and remember. (*Pause*) And remember me.

Doris At least you're not wounded inside.

Pause

Rosie (*removing another marble*) Look, this is a magic marble, when you hold it up to the sun there's a frozen fountain inside.

Doris It seems no time since you were trying to push that up your nose. (*Pause*) I'm going to put our tea on. Can you pass my shoes?

Rosie I'll do it.

Doris No, it really is my turn.

Rosie Have you got me a birthday cake?

Doris Yes.

Rosie I love you, Doris.

Doris A long time since anyone's said that to me. (*Pause*) Sixty-one years, Jack and I were married. I don't think we liked each other very much (*Pause*) There's a letter here for you.

Rosie There's no address on it.

Doris It's from your mother. And I've kept it safe in my scrapbox, with Jack's letter, and Margaret's exercise book, and the drawings Jackie did when she was a little girl. (*Pause*) After Margaret took you to London, Jackie came to see me. Left some baby clothes, and asked me to give you this letter when you reached sixteen. Happy birthday. (*She kisses Rosie*)

Doris exits to the house

Rosie picks up the letter, opens it and reads. Towards the end:

Rosie "... I don't know if you'll ever love me as much as I love you. But one day you'll understand why I've done this to you, probably not until you are on your own yourself ..."

Jackie appears in her Art Dealer dress and sits on the swing

Rosie folds the letter and puts it in her pocket. She concentrates on the Solitaire board and completes the game with a few last moves, so that one marble is left in the centre hole

Solitaire! (*She calls*) Gran! Gran, guess what, I've discovered the secret, all by myself! Gran? I'll prove it to you, come and watch, I'm going to do it all over again now, so that I remember it always. You there Gran? Gran ... ? (*Silence*) Oh never mind.

Rosie puts the headphones back on and hums quietly. She replaces all the marbles on the board

Margaret appears upstage in the distance, dressed as in her office (Act III, Scene Two). The blue kite flies up high over Margaret

Black-out

SCENE 8

Doris enters in the 1920s print dress which Jackie pulled from the box in Act II and a straw hat trimmed with flowers. She is breathless and her hair is awry. It is May 1923

Doris Mother! Mother? Oh, what do you think! It's happened, happened to me! All the way back on the train I could hardly keep still, I don't know what the other passengers must've thought, but I wouldn't be ladylike. Mother! Come and look. Do I look different? I must look different, I feel as though I've swallowed a firework. Oh it was a lovely, lovely day. We took a picnic, climbed up to the Waterloo Memorial, sat in the sunshine and it was after we'd finished the egg and cress; he couldn't wait till after the fruit cake! I felt so—shy, suddenly—I had to just stare and stare at the tablecloth while he was asking, blue and yellow squares, there was an ant struggling to carry a piece of cress across the corner ... These are things you remember all your life, I suppose. I didn't think it would be like this. (*Pause*) And then we just ran and ran! Talked, made plans, I felt somehow—weedy! (*She laughs*)—Sort of silly, for having given in ... to—love!—Do you know what I mean? (*Silence*) Mother? We ate your fruit cake on the train, Jack put a paper down so as not to drop crumbs on the velvet upholstery, but then he sat on a strawberry—and oh, I got a grass stain on my frock, but Jack says he'll buy me a new one. *And*, Mother, *and* I got promoted to Head of Infants this morning! Miss Butterworth called me into her office, my heart was in my mouth, I thought she was going to tick me off for this dress being too short! ... Jack was very proud when I told him, but of course he says I shan't need to work when we're—when we're—oh, of course he's going to ask you first, he's waiting in the front room, I opened the curtains so the neighbours can see—Oh and—

The lights begin to fade

I've seen just the posy, tiny white flowers, in the window of Ambleton's ... Oh Mother, I'm so happy, SO HAPPY! I suppose, really and truly, this is the beginning of my life!

The lights fade to a single spot on Doris, then snap out

FURNITURE AND PROPERTY LIST

On stage throughout: tub of geraniums

On stage throughout Acts I and II: baby grand piano and piano stool.

ACT I

SCENE 1

On stage: Black dustsheet completely covering piano. *On piano, under dustsheet:* sheet music. *On top of piano:* vase of white wax Christmas roses with red bow, lamp. *Underneath piano:* blankets, old-fashioned sleeping bag, bolster, stone hot water bottle, gas mask
Wireless

Waste ground:
Sweet wrappers

Off stage: Duster **(Doris)**

SCENE 2

Off stage: Doll, Christmas stocking **(Margaret)**
Floral overall, Utility-ware mug **(Doris)**

SCENE 3

Strike: Vase of wax flowers, lamp, wireless

Off stage: Plastic carrier bag. *In it:* large sanitary towel, kitchen funnel **(Rosie)**

SCENE 4

Strike: Carrier bag, sanitary towel, funnel, sweet wrappers

Set: Cherry tree in tub
Swing

Off stage: Red transistor radio **(Jackie)**
Tea towel **(Margaret)**

SCENE 5

Strike: Cherry tree, swing, transistor radio

Set: Child's painting of a tree
Pot of paint

Off stage: Chair, rug, tea tray. *On it:* cups, saucers, spoons, teapot, milk, sugar, cakes
            (Doris)
            Kendal mint cake **(Margaret)**

SCENE 6

Strike: Paint pot, chair, rug, tea tray, mint cake

Set: Worn piece of red carpet. *On it:* ashtrays, mugs, red transistor radio from
        Act I, Scene Four (*now worn and battered*)
        Three-month-old baby in Moses basket
        Two red baby socks
        Baby clothes (*including a dress with rabbits on it*)
        Holdall
        Plastic carrier bag. *In it:* feeding bottles, powdered milk
        Second plastic carrier bag. *In it:* baby clothes

Off stage: Sheet bundled up to look like a baby **(Margaret)**

SCENE 7

Strike: Carpet, ashtrays, mugs, transistor radio, one red baby sock, carrier bag
          containing baby clothes

Set: Sheets, socks and other washing (*strewn on ground*)
        Folded washing in washing basket

SCENE 8

Strike: Washing, washing basket

Off stage: Skipping rope **(Rosie)**
            Penknife **(Jackie)**

SCENE 9

Strike: Skipping rope, penknife

Set: Two telephones
        Moses basket

SCENE 10

Strike: Two telephones, Moses basket

Set: Cherry tree in tub (*now grown*)
        Swing
        Painting materials
        Child's painting

Off stage: Old spoon, doll (*like the one from Act I, Scene Two but now bald except for
            a few tufts which have been spiked, and naked except for one red sock*)
            (Rosie)
            Red baby sock, lavish birthday cake with candles, matches, cheque, gift-
            wrapped package containing lace **(Jackie)**
            Tray with drinks **(Margaret)**

ACT II

Strike: Cherry tree, swing, painting materials, spoon, doll, cake, matches, pack-
             age with lace, cheque, drinks tray

Set: French windows. *Outside them:* rose bush with snow on it
             Door to hall
             Dustsheet over piano. *Under the dustsheet:* silver salver
             Boxes covered with dustsheets
             Newspapers
             Packing tape
             Stepladder
             Dresser covered with dustsheet. *On the lower shelves:* willow pattern
             dinner service and, behind this, the Utility mug from Act I, Scene Two.
             On the upper shelves: silver rose bowl, old chocolate box containing
             framed photograph, other ornaments and framed photographs

Off stage: Flashlight, white rose, sheet with holes for eyes, round wooden Solitaire
             board **(Rosie)**
             Feather duster, bin liner containing curtains and baby clothes (*including
             the "rabbit" dress from Act I, Scene Six*) **(Doris)**
             Bin liner containing clothes (*including Jackie's flared jeans from Act I,
             Scene Four and Margaret's ski pants and Doris's beige skirt from Act I,
             Scene Seven*), holdall (*containing Thermos flask of tea, tin of polish,
             dusters, rubber gloves*) **(Margaret)**
             Boxes, bin liners **(Jackie)**

ACT III

Scene 1

Strike: French windows, door, rose bush, stepladder, dresser, boxes

Set: Bag of potting compost
             Tub (*to plant geraniums in*)

Off stage: Tray of small geraniums in pots **(Margaret)**

Scene 2

Strike: Bag of compost, tray with flower pots, newly planted tub

Set: Desk. *On it:* telephone, typewriter with cover, pot of geraniums, photo
             frame

Off stage: Orange kite, bundle of letters **(Rosie)**
             Chinese lacquered briefcase, blue kite **(Jackie)**

Personal: Tissues **(Margaret**, page 53)

Scene 3

Strike: Desk and contents, blue kite

Set: Twigs

SCENE 4

Strike: Twigs

SCENE 5

Set: Cherry tree
             Swing
             Photo
             Documents
             Red transistor radio

Off Stage: Chinese briefcase **(Jackie)**

SCENE 6

Strike: Cherry tree, swing, photo, documents, red transistor, briefcase

No props required

SCENE 7

Set: Two deckchairs
             Piano stool (*from Acts I and II*). *On it:* Solitaire board
             Yellow kite

Off stage: Kite tail **(Doris)**
             Blue kite **(Margaret)**

Personal: Walkman headphones **(Rosie)**
             Mirrored sunglasses, letter **(Doris)**

SCENE 8

Strike: Two deckchairs, piano stool, Solitaire board, kite

LIGHTING PLOT

ACT I, SCENE 1

To open: Lights up on waste ground

Cue 1	**Margaret** and **Rosie:** "After me." *Lights dim*	(Page 3)
Cue 2	**Margaret** and **Rosie:** "Amen." *Lights darken*	(Page 3)
Cue 3	**Jackie:** "YOU from behind the grave! Tell us how to kill Mummy!" *Lights almost black out*	(Page 3)
Cue 4	**Doris** begins to dust piano *Lights begin to rise; snap on lamp on piano*	(Page 3)

ACT I, SCENE 2

To open: Lights as for a front room on a winter's evening

Cue 5	**Margaret:** "Yes." *Lights fade from here on*	(Page 6)
Cue 6	**Margaret:** "... You're eight years old." *Black-out*	(Page 6)
Cue 7	**Doris** returns with a floral overall over her clothes *Lights up bright, as for a May day*	(Page 7)
Cue 8	**Jackie** and **Doris** go off together *Lights dim*	(Page 8)

ACT I, SCENE 3

To open: Lights up on waste ground

Cue 9	**Rosie:** "You have to get married first." *Black-out*	(Page 10)

ACT I, SCENE 4

To open: Exterior lighting

Cue 10	**Margaret** goes into the house *Blackout*	(Page 12)

ACT I, SCENE 5

To open: "Daylight"

Cue 11	**Doris** takes the painting	(Page 14)
	Black-out	

ACT I, SCENE 6

To open: Winter "daylight"

Cue 12	**Jackie:** "Mummy, Mummy!"	(Page 17)
	Black-out	
Cue 13	Baby starts crying	(Page 17)
	Dim light	
Cue 14	**Margaret:** "It's all right ... ssh ... ssh ..."	(Page 18)
	Lights up brightly	

ACT I, SCENE 7

To open: Summer "daylight"

Cue 15	**Doris** drops basket and surveys spoiled washing as sound of	(Page 21)
	rain grows louder	
	Black-out	

ACT I, SCENE 8

To open: Lights up on waste ground area

Cue 16	**Rosie:** "You mustn't ever break a vow."	(Page 22)
	Black-out	

ACT I, SCENE 9

To open: Lights up on **Margaret** and **Doris**

Cue 17	**Margaret:** "Jackie, what are you doing ...!"	(Page 24)
	Black-out on Margaret and Doris	

ACT I, SCENE 10

To open: Daylight

Cue 18	**Jackie** puts sock on doll	(Page 28)
	Black-out	

ACT II, SCENE 1

To open: Winter daylight

Cue 19	**Doris:** "I doubt it."	(Page 29)
	Lights up bright, suddenly	
Cue 20	**Doris:** "... put your anorak on."	(Page 44)
	Snap off light on living-room area	

Cue 21   Sound of wind and snow blizzard up full   (Page 45)
            Black-out

ACT III, SCENE 1

To open: Spring daylight

No cues

ACT III, SCENE 2

To open: Bright sunny morning

Cue 22   **Margaret** exits   (Page 53)
            Black-out

ACT III, SCENE 3

To open: Almost dark

No cues

ACT III, SCENE 4

To open: Spring daylight

Cue 23   **Margaret:** "... if I just keep going."   (Page 55)
            Lights fade

Cue 24   Sound of baby and child crying   (Page 55)
            Fade out

ACT III, SCENE 5

To open: Early morning spring light

Cue 25   **Rosie** walks away   (Page 58)
            Lights fade to black-out

ACT III, SCENE 6

To open: Exterior lighting

Cue 26   **Margaret** and **Jackie** run off together   (Page 58)
            Lights fade

ACT III, SCENE 7

To open: Sunlight

Cue 27   Blue kite flies up high over **Margaret**   (Page 63)
            Black-out

ACT III, SCENE 8

Cue 28   **Doris:** "... neighbours can see—Oh and—"   (Page 63)
            Begin to fade lights

Cue 29   **Doris:** "... beginning of my life!"   (Page 63)
            Fade lights to a single spot on Doris, then snap out

EFFECTS PLOT

ACT I

Cue 1   **Doris** begins to dust piano   (Page 4)
On the wireless: George Formby's "Chinese Laundry Blues"

Cue 2   **Doris** turns off the wireless   (Page 4)
Cut music on wireless

Cue 3   **Margaret** resumes playing   (Page 5)
Sound of a distant air-raid siren

Cue 4   **Margaret:** "I *know*, I—Sukey thinks—"   (Page 5)
*Distant rumble of aeroplanes which continues through the rest of
    the scene*

Cue 5   **Doris:** exits   (Page 6)
Fade sound of aeroplane

Cue 6   **Doris** returns, lights come up bright   (Page 7)
Birdsong

Cue 7   **Doris:** "... I brought you some cocoa."   (Page 8)
Sound of distant aeroplanes

Cue 8   As Scene three opens   (Page 8)
Sound of two cats wailing like babies

Cue 9   **Rosie** runs in   (Page 9)
Cut cats wailing

Cue 10   As Scene Four opens   (Page 11)
Music on radio: "All You Need Is Love" (Beatles), loud

Cue 11   **Jackie:** "You sound like Granny now." *She switches the radio*   (Page 11)
off
Cut music

Cue 12   As Scene five opens   (Page 12)
Sound of lawnmower, off right

Cue 13   **Doris:** "Jack! Jack!"   (Page 12)
Cut lawnmower

Cue 14   **Doris:** "... Margaret can't stop long."   (Page 12)
Pause, then start lawnmower sound again

Cue 15   **Doris:** "... clippings in our tea."   (Page 12)
Lawnmower fades away to right

Cue 16   As Scene six opens   (Page 14)
*Baby crying. Over this blares out the sound of a transistor radio:
    1971 Manchester DJ, first weather forecast, commentary, etc.,
    then music: "Honkey Tonk Woman" (Rolling Stones)*

Cue 17	**Jackie:** "... it won't all go in!" *Baby yells*	(Page 14)
Cue 18	**Jackie** hits the transistor radio *Cut transistor radio*	(Page 14)
Cue 19	**Jackie:** "Ssh, Rosie, please—" *Baby yells*	(Page 14)
Cue 20	**Jackie:** "Shut up!" *Cut baby crying, abruptly*	(Page 14)
Cue 21	**Jackie:** "... little basket." *Baby coos*	(Page 15)
Cue 22	**Jackie:** "Sleep, beautiful ... ssh ..." *Baby makes little cry*	(Page 15)
Cue 23	**Jackie** dangles the red sock over the baby *Baby quietens during the rest of Jackie's speech*	(Page 15)
Cue 24	**Margaret:** "You think I don't know?" *Baby coos softly*	(Page 16)
Cue 25	**Margaret:** "Ssh, there now." *Baby murmurs*	(Page 16)
Cue 26	**Jackie:** "... like an apricot ..." *Baby makes snuffling noise*	(Page 16)
Cue 27	Black-out *Sound of baby crying*	(Page 17)
Cue 28	**Margaret:** "There now, there now, hush ... nasty dream?" *Baby quietens down during this speech, coos and then is silent*	(Page 17)
Cue 29	As Scene seven opens *Distant rumble of thunder; sound of tennis game, off*	(Page 18)
Cue 30	**Doris:** "... in the middle." *Sound of light aircraft overhead*	(Page 18)
Cue 31	**Margaret:** "I'm in love, Mother." *Distant rumble of thunder*	(Page 18)
Cue 32	**Margaret:** "... Ken and I have decided." *Distant rumble of thunder*	(Page 19)
Cue 33	**Doris:** "... why does it have to be London?" *Sound of a raucous car horn, which repeats*	(Page 20)
Cue 34	**Doris:** "... get the best service out." *Rumble of thunder, close*	(Page 21)
Cue 35	**Doris** picks up the basket and walks towards the house *Crack of thunder overhead*	(Page 21)
Cue 36	**Doris** drops the basket *Sound of pouring rain on leaves; grows louder*	(Page 21)
Cue 37	**Margaret:** "... I was just seeing to ..." *Baby cries in the distance*	(Page 23)

MADE AND PRINTED IN GREAT BRITAIN BY
LATIMER TREND & COMPANY LTD PLYMOUTH

MADE IN ENGLAND